My Shanghai

Through tastes & memories

My Shanghai

Through tastes & memories

Sandy Lam

TIMES EDITIONS

Art Direction : David Yip
Designer : Christopher Wong
Photographer : Edmond Ho
Text : Tan Dawn Wei, Stephen Lee

Published by Times Editions – Marshall Cavendish
International (Asia) Private Limited
A member of Times Publishing Limited
Times Centre, 1 New Industrial Road, Singapore 536196
Tel: (65) 6213 9288   Fax: (65) 6285 4871
E-mail: te@sg.marshallcavendish.com
On-line Bookstore: http://www.timesone.com.sg/te

Malaysian Office:
Federal Publications Sdn Berhad
(General & Reference Publishing) (3024-D)
Times Subang, Lot 46, Persiaran Teknologi Subang
Subang Hi-Tech Industrial Park, Batu Tiga,
40000 Shah Alam
Selangor Darul Ehsan, Malaysia
Tel: (603) 5635 2191   Fax: (603) 5635 2706
E-mail: cchong@tpg.com.my

**National Library Board Singapore Cataloguing in
Publication Data**

Lam, Sandy, 1966
My Shanghai : through tastes & memories / Sandy Lam.
Singapore : Times Editions, c2004.
p. cm.
ISBN : 981-232-832-7

1. Lam, Sandy, 1966 2. Women singers—China – Hong Kong –
Biography. 3. Cookery, Chinese. 4. Cookery—China – Shanghai.
I. Title.

TX724.5.C5   641.5951132 — dc21
SLS2004010742

Printed in Singapore.

Dedicated to the loving memory of
my mother and grandmother

Contents

Celebrity Chefs

Ah Niang, *Taihe Yinshi Dian*
Jereme Leung, *Whampoa Club,*
Three on the Bund
Paul Hsu, *Ye Shanghai*
He Shuiying, *Jiajia Tang Bao Dian*
Susumu Fukui, *La Villa Rouge*
Qian Shixian, *Sophia's Tea & Restaurant*
Uncle Li, *Shanghai Uncle*

Recipes

Recipes

Jereme Leung,
Whampoa Club, Three on the Bund

Paul Hsu,
Ye Shanghai

Recipes

Susumu Fukui,
La Villa Rouge

· Shanghainese Crab, Avocado and Celeriac
  Timbale Salad with Aromatic Balsamic Sauce
  accompanied by Beluga Caviar 146

Recipes

A city and its cuisine

On the banks of the Yangtze River

Since its beginnings in the 18th century, Shanghai has been famed as a meeting point of cultures.

The city's strategic location, hugging the south bank of the mighty Yangtze River, has made it, since its earliest days, an important port-of-call and commercial centre.

Traders, merchants, workers and fortune seekers from all over China and as far away as Portugal, England, France, Russia and Japan gravitated to the city. Some visited, some chose to stay. They filled the streets with their merchandise and exotic cultures, and imbued the city with an elegant, cosmopolitan flavour.

Along with them, they brought their culinary traditions.

The making of a cuisine

Over the years, the chefs of Shanghai have absorbed and adapted the best of these, no matter their origins—Western, wealthy Chinese or common working class—because the Shanghainese believe good food does not discriminate. The result was a gastronomic melting pot of diverse flavours and styles.

Thus, was Shanghainese cuisine born.

However, apart from tradition and heritage, its climate, geography and regional influences also helped shape Shanghainese cuisine.

In a city surrounded by river, lake and sea, seafood naturally became a main ingredient. Best known of these, perhaps, is the freshwater hairy crab, whose arrival every autumn is a major event on the city's epicurean calendar.

Shanghai is also home to the drunken crab: marinated in rice wine and served raw. Yellow fish too, is found on practically every menu across the city, as is eel—from the rough-and-ready roadside stall frequented by the locals, to the swankiest restaurant where the expatriates dine.

Shanghai's northern climate has its effects too. Cold winters see oilier, sweeter and heavier tastes predominate, as compared to the lighter flavours of the south, while the hot summers are largely responsible for 'cooling' dishes made from soybean as well as preserved food like salted meats and pickles.

The weather aside, many traits of Shanghainese cooking come from the style of home cooking of neighbouring Zhejiang and Jiangsu provinces. Chief among these are the heavy tastes, glistening textures and sweet sauces so characteristic of Shanghainese cuisine, as are the favoured cooking methods of braising, stewing and quick-frying.

New promises

The new Shanghai sits at an even larger crossroads of cultures—and cuisines.

Since China re-opened its doors to the world in 1979, the city has undergone a quiet culinary revolution. Today, more than 10,000 restaurants cater to every possible palate and ambience.

Healthy eating is a noticeable trend, and many restaurants have lightened up—reducing their salt and oil content and their once-hefty portions, and in the process, ushering in a new era of Shanghainese cuisine.

But while trends and change abound, thankfully so do traditions. And if you are in search of the authentic flavours and feel of Old Shanghai, you will still find it with ease amidst the city's feverish rush to modernisation. For East will always meet West, the old meet the new, and eating will always be unforgettable, in this ever-surprising metropolis on the Yangtze.

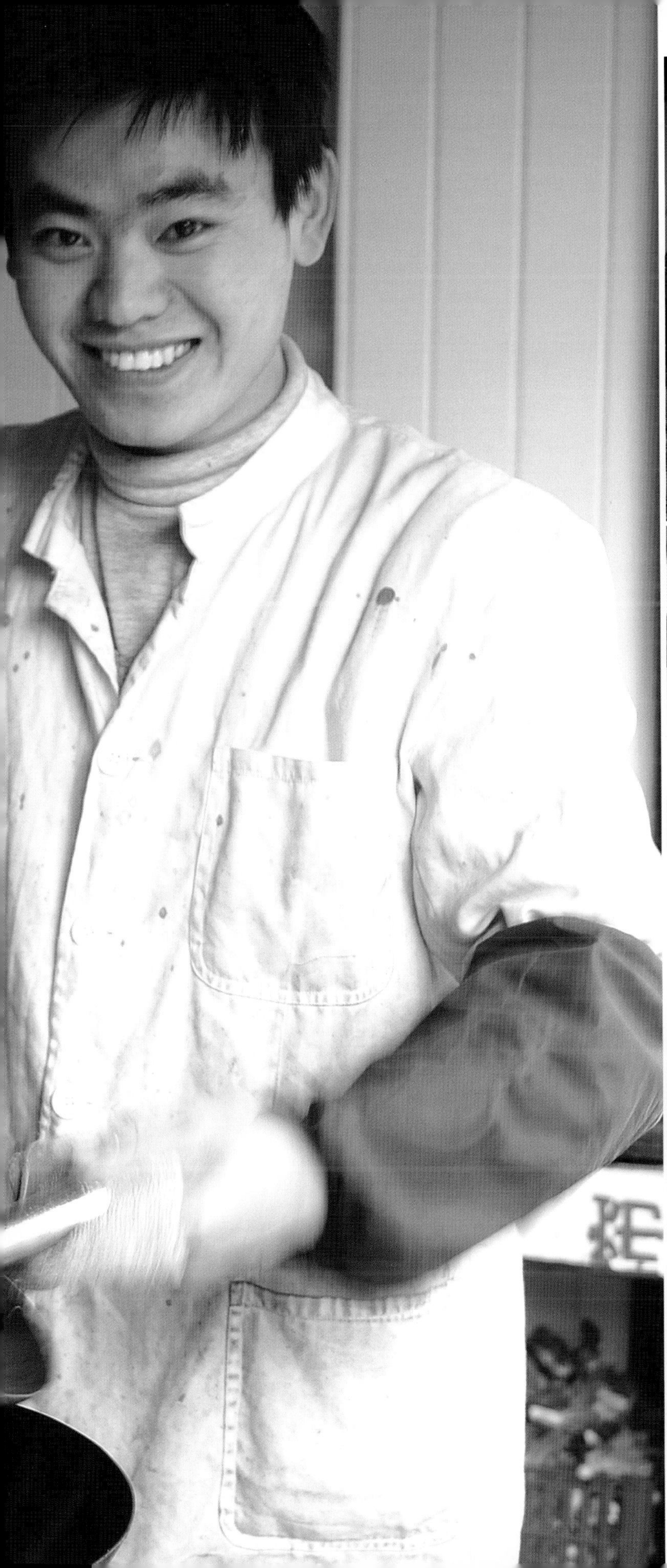

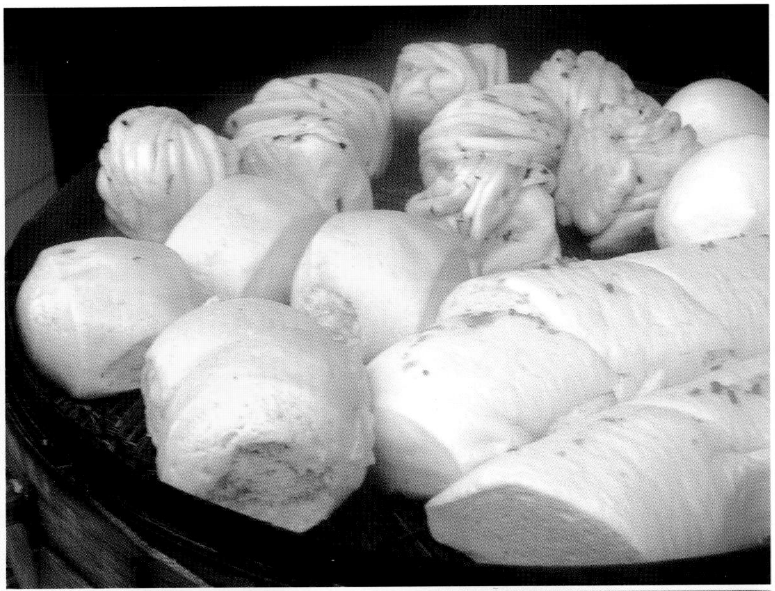

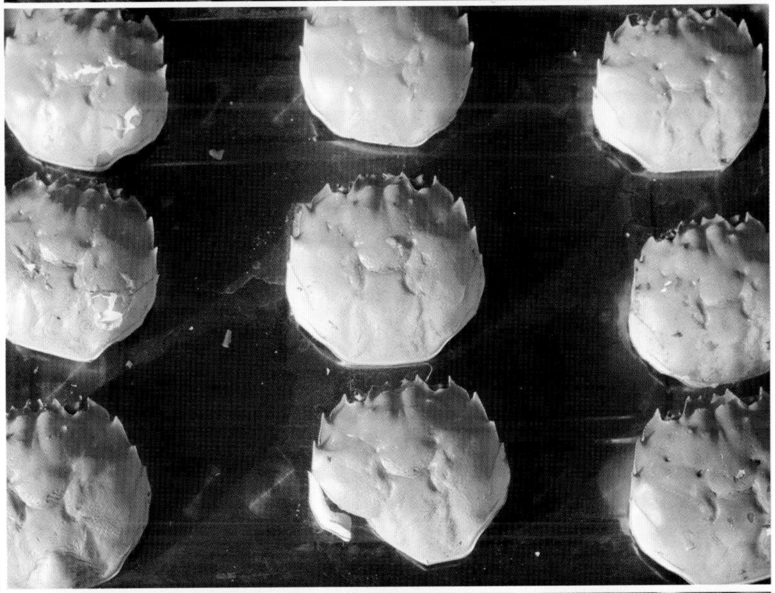

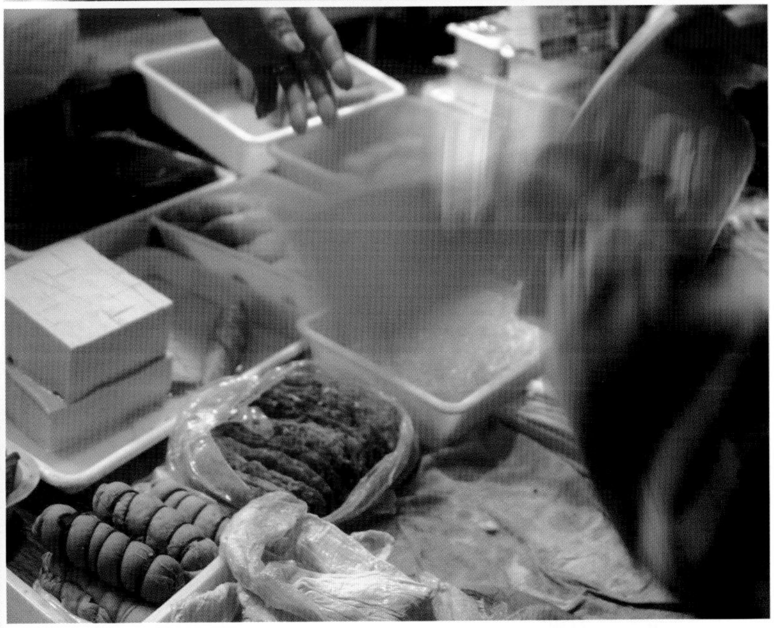

How do you taste life?

First flavours

The tastes we grow up with are often the ones which stay with us for life. We reminisce about them and often try to re-capture them, for they remind us of an innocent and carefree time in our past—our childhood. These tastes have become for us, a manner of comfort food.

Me, I've always had a yearning for the 'real' Shanghainese taste. Although I was born and raised in Hong Kong, Shanghainese food is intimately linked to my sense of identity and my childhood memories.

My birthplace at North Point, Hong Kong, was an enclave of the Shanghainese and Hokkien. There were five members in my family and we lived in a small rented room in an apartment block. We had a radio cassette recorder in our room and the landlady's television set in the common hallway by way of entertainment. I remember sitting by my family's radio after school, in the gloomy half-light of the room, waiting breathlessly for my favourite song to come on.

But my life, even then, was suffused with the scent of the stove. We, along with all the families who lived on the same floor, had to share one kitchen. So, naturally, around mealtimes each day, a parade of smells would waft through the corridors and rooms. We

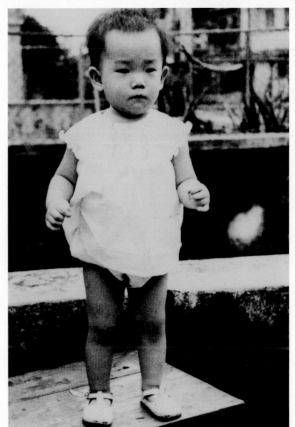

My birthplace, North Point in Hong Kong, also known as 'Little Shanghai'. At 18 months (top), and with mum and a younger brother (bottom).

More memories of North Point. These photos are the products of my father's hobby—and his dark room at home! At 5 years of age (main photo).

became quite adept—my brothers and I—at deciphering the dish by its aroma. I suppose destiny ordained, from early on, that food would loom large in my life!

But my initiation was just beginning. I grew up in a home where meals were a mix of Shanghainese and Cantonese. My grandma is Cantonese, and my dad loves Shanghainese food. So a typical meal will have something very traditionally Shanghainese, like fried freshwater prawns, and something very Cantonese like melon vermicelli.

The refrigerator and the kitchen

I came to love these dishes, as I did granny's pork chops with potatoes, which I miss the most. I miss not just the flavours that granny weaved with her food, but her portions. They were so ample they filled the table and kept us going for days! There would be meat, there would be soup—Russian Borscht or some steaming Cantonese soup. There would be red-braised fish—either yellow croaker or pomfret —and a stir-fried vegetable. I remember raiding the refrigerator up to three days later, my brothers and I; we'd eat the leftovers cold, and they'd be just as yummy.

My mother, on the other hand, made the best of wontons and had a wonderfully quirky habit. She would come home from a memorable meal and excitedly set about trying to recreate her latest gastronomic experience in the kitchen—much to my delight of course. And how could I not mention my favourite place in the whole house—our kitchen? Humble and small our kitchen may

have been, but to me, it was grand with significance. My passion for food and cooking grew out of it. Whenever granny started the wok and I caught the whiff of garlic and spring onions being fried, I'd literally dash in.

Clutching at ghosts

Ever since then, and wherever I might be, I've tried to keep the memory and sensations of that childhood kitchen alive; except that these days I would be wearing the apron, and the results would invariably be mixed. On good days, I might think I almost had those magical tastes and aromas with me again; on bad days, they might as well have been ghosts.

In one's memories, things always taste better.

And I slowly began to see why.

Cooking is a unique and personal process. No dish tastes exactly the same twice. A hundred and one things can affect the outcome—the freshness of the ingredients, the temperature, the sauce you use, even the weather. My parents and grandmother cooked by feel, not with a measuring cup. I realised in my heart of hearts I was asking the impossible.

A different angle

So when I was asked to do this book, I had mixed feelings. Shanghai is a city I love, but my experience of it, as far as my nostalgic search for flavours went, has been bittersweet—like my fortunes in my own kitchen. When I first arrived in Shanghai almost fifteen years ago, I naturally

The other 'members' of my family: with a neighbour's thoughtful-looking pooch (top); my 'doggy' jumper and me (bottom left), with brother and 'Lucky' at Victoria Park in Hong Kong (bottom right).

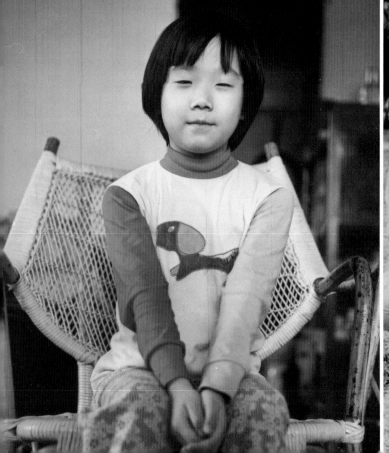

scoured its restaurants and stalls... but the flavours of my childhood just weren't there anymore.

Like everything else, cuisines and tastes evolve. Shanghai is no different; the city—and its cuisine—has changed. Now that Shanghai has gained itself a reputation, and has started to attract the food elite from around the world, its cuisine is understandably heading in new — even experimental—directions. My humble home-grown quest just didn't stand a chance.

Or so I thought until my parents themselves returned to Shanghai some years later. Using ingredients that were authentically Shanghainese—even to the soy sauce and oil— they brought my childhood kitchen as close as it had ever been, to life again.

We all learn somehow

So as a personal food journey, Shanghai has been a series of ups-and-downs, hits-and-misses for me. However, through my stomach —or should I say greed?—I've learned a few things about life. One is that things never stay the same, and that's why our memories are especially precious and ought to be cherished, because they can never be perfectly re-lived.

Another thing I've learned is that, while certain tastes may have vanished, the *love* of good food never does. And that is what I celebrate in this book, by featuring flavours and recipes both old and new, and culinary discoveries I've made in Shanghai.

I believe that good food is one of the greatest joys and pleasures of life, something that can

be enjoyed by everyone, regardless of one's station in life. This is borne out by the chefs and restaurant owners who have shared with us, so generously, their knowledge and passion for their art—and inspired me without end. And most vividly by the unforgettable Ah Niang, who served her bowls of noodles from her rather rudimentary kitchen, and—might I add—from her heart.

All these, I have tried to convey in this book.

Resolution

Finally, while I do regret not taking the time to learn more about cooking from granny and my mother while they were still around, I'm at least glad my daughter had the opportunity to live in Shanghai for the past two and a half years. She will remember Shanghainese dishes like niangao (rice cake), and kaofu (wheat gluten), which is her favourite. She will share with me an experience that might otherwise not have materialised had she grown up in Taiwan or Hong Kong. An experience that I hope will give her as much delight and meaning in her life as it has given me in mine.

This book is therefore about love and remembering, and the enrichment of life that food brings. My grandmother and my parents passed on to me a love for good food. I grew up eating well and loving it... how blessed could a person be? These flavours and memories are mine for life.

Childhood Nostalgia

Grandma in her 'cheongsam' in early 30s Shanghai. She cared for me since I was young and I'd like to think that some of her free-spirited character rubbed off on me!

Grandma's exquisite pork chops

In Shanghainese, potatoes are called 'yang shan yu'. They were my brother's favourite, as well as mine—whether made into French fries, potato soup, potato salad or minced meat potato pancakes.

Pork chops with potatoes was a common dish on our family's dining table. And it's something my brother and I often reminisce about nowadays. We'd recall our grandma's pork chops, how they kept in the fridge for days, and how they were a big part of our childhood. We'd argue also over how best to re-create this dish, and enjoy once more the tastes we used to know.

My grandma was from Shunde, Guangdong. Although she spent most of her life in Shanghai, her style of cooking remained strictly Cantonese. She would always ask the butcher to de-bone the meat and cut them into big pieces. When she brought them home, she'd cut them further into portions about two fingers wide.

Grandma would soak the potatoes in water for an hour. She'd say it was important to do that to get rid of the starch. She would pat them dry and fry them to a crisp golden brown.

In true Cantonese style, grandma's pork chops were never oily nor cloying; they were always fresh and tender, and the potatoes, which absorbed the sweetness of the meat, had a texture which melted in your mouth. The longer it kept, the better the dish tasted. We often left it in the fridge for up to three days, and it would still taste amazing, even when eaten cold.

Pork Chops with Potatoes

INGREDIENTS

Pork chops
6 pieces

Cooking oil
2 cups

Potatoes
3, peeled and cut into thick strips.
Soak in salted water for $1/2$ hour,
drain

Spring onions
2 stalks, cut into 4-cm lengths

Chicken stock
$1/2$ cup

Seasoning:

Light soy sauce
1 Tbsp

Dark soy sauce
1 Tbsp

Sugar
1 tsp

Cornstarch
1 Tbsp

Chinese wine
1 Tbsp

Sesame oil
$1/2$ tsp

METHOD

- Season pork chops and leave to marinate for 30 minutes.

- Heat oil in a wok. Deep-fry potatoes until slightly brown. Drain and set aside.

- Heat 1 Tbsp oil and stir-fry 1 stalk spring onion till fragrant. Add pork chops and brown each side.

- Add potatoes and mix thoroughly.

- Add $1/2$ cup chicken stock and 1 stalk spring onion and simmer for 5–10 minutes. Serve hot.

洋山芋烧排骨

Deep-fried Pork Chops

INGREDIENTS

Pork chops
8 pieces, bone removed

Eggs
3, beaten

Breadcrumbs
2 cups

Cooking oil
2 cups

Tomato sauce
for dip

Seasoning:

Salt
1 tsp

Five-spice powder
1 tsp

Cornstarch
1 Tbsp

METHOD

• Season pork chops and leave to marinate.

• Beat 3 eggs thoroughly in a bowl.

• Pour breadcrumbs out on to a plate.

• Heat 2 cups of oil in a frying pan.

• Dip pork chops in beaten egg, then coat with breadcrumbs.

• Deep-fry pork chops in heated oil till golden brown.

• Serve hot with tomato sauce

黄金猪排

Deep-fried Garoupa

INGREDIENTS

Garoupa
12 fillets

Eggs
3

Breadcrumbs
1 cup

Cooking oil
2 cups

Lemon
$^1/_2$, cut into wedges

Mayonnaise
4 Tbsp

Seasoning:

Salt
1 tsp

Five-spice powder
1 tsp

Cornstarch
1 Tbsp

METHOD

- Season fish fillets and leave to marinate for 10–15 minutes.

- Beat eggs thoroughly in a bowl. Set aside.

- Pour breadcrumbs out on to a plate.

- Heat oil for deep-frying.

- Dip fish in egg mixture, then coat evenly with breadcrumbs.

- Fry fish till golden brown.

- Serve hot with wedges of lemon and mayonnaise.

Ming Yuen West Street, North Point, was my neighbourhood and playground. Here, I'm with my brother and grandma, who's in her fifties.

The delights of Chinese New Year

I would always remember the buzz of activity in our kitchen come Chinese New Year. My grandmother would become a super woman toiling away in our dimly lit kitchen, preparing the carrot cake, sweet soup, steamed chicken, fried fish and deep-fried yam fritters, that would make our reunion dinner.

When she had finished, she would offer incense and thank the gods before we sat down to our meal—which would make us kids the happiest.

I loved squatting by the kitchen and watching grandma make egg dumplings. She said that these dumplings represented gold ingots, and so they were must-haves every new year. Egg dumplings are made from fresh egg pancakes and a pinch of minced pork. And the way they were made—or at least the way grandma used to make them—always looked fun.

She would sit on a stool by the stove and heat a stainless steel ladle over the fire. In would go a piece of lard which would crackle as it melted and coated the inside of the ladle. Grandma would then pour in the egg mixture and gently swirl it into a thin pancake in the ladle. She would place a pinch of minced pork in the centre, fold the pancake, and roll it into a little package to look like a plump yellow nugget. The soup was made from Chinese ham, old chicken and Chinese cabbage.

To put those egg dumplings in my mouth—and taste the essence of the chicken soup and the sweetness of the Chinese cabbage absorbed in the folds of that yellow skin—was one of the highlights of the reunion meal for me.

But the New Year dish I never learned from grandma was the deep-fried yam fritters. Because it needed deep-frying in oil, she never allowed me in the kitchen to watch for fear of splatter; so its finer points of preparation have forever escaped me—that is one of my biggest culinary regrets.

Cabbage with Egg Dumplings Soup

Pork
500g, minced

Cooking oil
5 Tbsp

Eggs
3

Salt
1/2 tsp

Sesame oil
1/4 tsp

Chicken stock
3 cups

Beijing cabbage (Jinbai)
1, cut into large pieces

Vermicelli
100g, soaked in water until soft

Spring onions
2 stalks, finely chopped

Seasoning:

Ginger
1 tsp, finely grated

Spring onion
2 stalks, finely chopped

Salt
1/2 tsp

Light soy sauce
1 tsp

Rice wine
1 tsp

Cornstarch
2 tsp

Egg
1, white only

White pepper
to taste

Sesame oil
1/2 tsp

METHOD

- Mix minced pork with seasoning ingredients. Set aside about one-third of it for the egg dumplings. Shape the rest into meat balls. Heat the oil and lightly brown the meat balls. Remove and set aside.

- To prepare egg dumplings, beat eggs thoroughly with salt and sesame oil. Heat an aluminium ladle over low heat. When hot, put a bit of oil and 1 tsp of egg mixture in the ladle. Swirl the egg mixture in the ladle until a thin pancake forms. Put some meat in the centre of the pancake and fold the pancake into two. Flip over and set aside. Continue with the rest of the batter.

- Heat chicken stock, add Beijing cabbage and boil till soft.

- Add meatballs and egg dumplings and cook for 10 minutes.

- Add vermicelli and garnish with chopped spring onions.

- Serve hot.

砂锅津白

Shanghai Niangao in Soup with Pork and Preserved Vegetables

INGREDIENTS

Cooking oil
2 Tbsp

Pork
100g, finely shredded

Spring onions
2 stalks, finely chopped

Ginger
1 Tbsp, finely shredded

Dried shrimps
20g, soaked and squeezed dry

Chinese wine
1 tsp

Preserved vegetables
50g, finely chopped

Chicken stock
3 cups

Sugar
1 tsp

Dried *niangao*
200g, soaked overnight

Seasoning:

Light soy sauce
1 Tbsp

Chinese wine
$^1/_2$ Tbsp

Sugar
$^1/_2$ tsp

Cornstarch
1 tsp

Sesame oil
$^1/_2$ tsp

METHOD

- Heat 1 Tbsp of oil and stir-fry shredded pork until slightly brown. Remove and set aside.

- Heat 1 Tbsp of oil and stir-fry spring onions and ginger until fragrant. Add dried shrimps and fry until fragrant. Drizzle with wine. Add preserved vegetables and fry until the oil is completely absorbed. Add shredded pork and continue to stir-fry. Add $^1/_4$ cup of chicken stock and simmer for 3 minutes. Add sugar and remove to a bowl.

- Boil the rest of the chicken stock in a medium-sized saucepan.

- Add *niangao* and cook until al dente. Add the desired amount of pork mixture and seasoning and serve immediately.

- Alternatively, you may replace *niangao* with rice noodles.

雪菜肉丝汤年糕

**With mum at home. I was
2 years old and in a rather
unsociable mood.**

Wondrous wontons!

On rainy days or when it is windy, I would think about eating wontons—they are comfort food to me. When I turned vegetarian for a couple of years in the past, I actually thought about possible recipes for good vegetarian wontons.

In my vegetarian phase, I was also plagued by fear whenever I visited my mother—fear of her formidable pork wontons. These would have been, quite honestly, a real test of my resolve, had I encountered them at mum's.

Such is the near-mystique of wontons among the Shanghainese. Wontons and noodles are, in fact, even more popular than rice as a staple here. Every family wraps wontons; most Shanghainese can wrap at least a hundred of these little bundles of joy at one sitting. My brother and I prefer to do justice to wontons with our stomachs—at the easy rate of at least 25 per sitting! And since wrapping wontons does take a lot of time, people would make surplus wontons and freeze them for future use.

There was a time when even the meat would be minced at home. The mix of lean meat to fat was extremely important and made the difference between a good and mediocre wonton. My mum loved watercress in her wontons; it was an unusual ingredient but gave the wonton a heightened flavour. Only when watercress was not available would my mother use cabbage.

I've eaten wontons at restaurants, but I don't quite fancy the rich chicken stock that they are served in. I only eat two of them these days—which says a lot about how much I miss the wontons of my childhood.

Shanghai Wonton Soup

INGREDIENTS

Watercress
2 cups, blanched in salt water, drained and squeezed dry. Finely chopped

Pork
1 cup, minced

Prawns
1 cup, shelled and deveined

Ginger
1 Tbsp, finely grated

Ginger juice
1 Tbsp

Spring onions
2 stalks, finely chopped

Wonton skins
30 pieces

Chicken stock
3 cups

Salt
$1/2$ Tbsp

Pepper
a pinch

Flour for dusting

Seasoning:

Light soy sauce
2 Tbsp

Salt
1 tsp

Sugar
$1/2$ tsp

Chinese wine
1 Tbsp

Sesame oil
$1/2$ tsp

Cornstarch
1 Tbsp

Pepper
a pinch

METHOD

- Put all ingredients, except wonton skins, chicken stock, salt and pepper, in a bowl. Add seasoning ingredients and mix thoroughly. Set aside.

- Place a piece of wonton skin on your palm. Put about $3/4$ Tbsp of meat mixture in the centre of the wonton skin. With your fingertips, wet the edge of the wonton skin and fold it into a rectangular shape. Put the wonton on a plate dusted with flour. Prepare the rest of the wontons.

- Boil 3 cups of water. Drop wontons into the boiling water. Cook for 5–10 minutes until the wontons float to the surface. Add $1/2$ cup of cold water and boil again. Once the water reboils, the wontons are cooked.

- Meanwhile, bring chicken stock to boil and season with salt and pepper.

- Serve the wontons in individual bowls with hot chicken stock. Garnish with spring onions and serve hot.

上海云吞

Vegetarian-style Wonton

INGREDIENTS

Cooking oil
2 Tbsp

Preserved vegetables
$^1/_2$ cup

Sesame oil
1 tsp

Ginger
1 Tbsp, finely grated with juice

Sugar
$^1/_2$ tsp

Watercress
1 cup, blanched in lightly salted water. Drain and squeeze dry. Chop finely.

Dried mushrooms
$^1/_2$ cup, soaked in water. Drain and chop finely.

Vermicelli
$^1/_3$ cup, soaked in water. Drain and chop finely.

Spring onions
$^1/_3$ cup, finely chopped

Omelette
$^1/_3$ cup, finely chopped

Wonton skins
30 pieces

Chicken broth
3 cups, seasoned with salt (optional)

Seasoning:

Oyster sauce
1 Tbsp

Chinese wine
1 Tbsp

Salt
$^1/_2$ tsp

METHOD

- Heat oil in a wok. Fry preserved vegetables with a dash of sesame oil, 1 tsp of ginger juice and sugar.

- Put all ingredients, except wonton skins, into a big bowl. Add seasoning and mix well.

- Divide the mixture into 30 portions.

- Place a piece of wonton skin flat on your palm and put a portion of the mixture in the centre of the wonton skin. Fold into halves to get a crescent shape. Bring the two ends together to overlap slightly. Moisten one end and paste the ends down firmly.

- Boil a saucepan of water. Drop wontons into boiling water. Remove the wontons when they float to the surface.

- Serve wontons in chicken broth garnished with sprigs of coriander or serve cold as an appetizer with a dip of vinegar and finely shredded ginger.

上海素云吞

Mum was an amateur
Shanghainese opera performer
(above); mum in her early 30s
(left)

Life's a feast with mum

They say there's a child in each of us; and to me, no truer example of this exists than my mother. The mere prospect of food—whether it's the eating, the cooking, or just the mention of it—was enough to reduce her normally shy and guarded personality to girlish giggles and flutters.

Only food had that effect on her, and in her later years, the adventure of food became the intimate bond between us. I'd offer to take her to a meal, and she'd make an event (gala, almost) of it. She'd preen and dress for the outing, and get all fluttery, and afterwards proudly make known to all her friends where 'Ah Lin' (that's me) had treated her. On those eating escapades, mum was not mum; she was my best friend.

In my school days when I had friends over, my mother would sometimes cook for us. Her drunken chicken and kaufu, two Shanghainese dishes she was especially good at, were always eagerly anticipated. When we ate, she would remain shyly in the kitchen, but our ecstatic 'oohs' and 'aahs'—clearly audible to her—would, I'm sure, have pleased her without end.

Anyway, I knew the cooking, alone, would have been reward enough for her. Nothing enraptured her more. The kitchen was her world and her space, and as long as she continued to churn out that fabulous drunken chicken and kaufu, I was glad to respect that!

But once, I remember, the family had to intervene. She was preparing the Smoked Grass Carp—one of dad's favourites. While filleting the fish with a cleaver, she cut her hand badly. As the blood dripped, all she said as she wiped it away was, "It's bleeding..." No tears, no complaints; she was one tough lady. Nevertheless, dad forbade my mom from ever cooking that dish again, and he learned to cook it himself.

There was, in those days at Causeway Bay, a local eatery known as Queen's Café, which served heavenly Potato Salad and Russian Borscht. We all loved them, mum included; so into the kitchen she went, on a mission we knew only too well.

She would fuss and mutter to herself over the stove for hours, be lost to the world and impatient with any intrusion, until, finally, the determined struggle over, she would emerge and announce with undisguised delight to the world her latest culinary triumphs—Potato Salad and Russian Borscht *ala* mum!

And so the family enjoyed many meals with the salad and the soup mum had 'reinterpreted', often accompanied by the sweetish Cantonese confection known as 'rib bread'. If there were a culinary obsession I inherited from mum, it would be the recapturing of tastes I had enjoyed.

My mother's zest for the pleasures of living shone brightest in the kitchen and at the dining table; for this and many other things, I truly miss her.

Drunken Chicken

INGREDIENTS

Chicken
1 (about 600g)

Spring onions
2 stalks, knotted

Ginger
5 slices

Coriander leaves
1 sprig

Seasoning:

Hua Tiao wine
2 cups

Chicken stock
3 cups

Salt
$1/2$ cup

METHOD

- Boil chicken, spring onions and ginger in a covered pot for 20–25 minutes.

- Get ready another pot of cold water with 1 Tbsp of salt. Remove chicken from hot broth and immerse it immediately in the cold water. Remove chicken when thoroughly cool.

- Strain chicken broth and add $1/2$ cup of salt. The broth should taste like seawater. Add 2 cups of Hua Tiao wine and let the broth cool to room temperature.

- Immerse chicken in broth to absorb the flavours for at least 8 hours.

- Remove chicken from broth and drain till completely dry.

- Cut chicken into bite-sized pieces and serve with shredded ginger and coriander leaves.

醉鸡

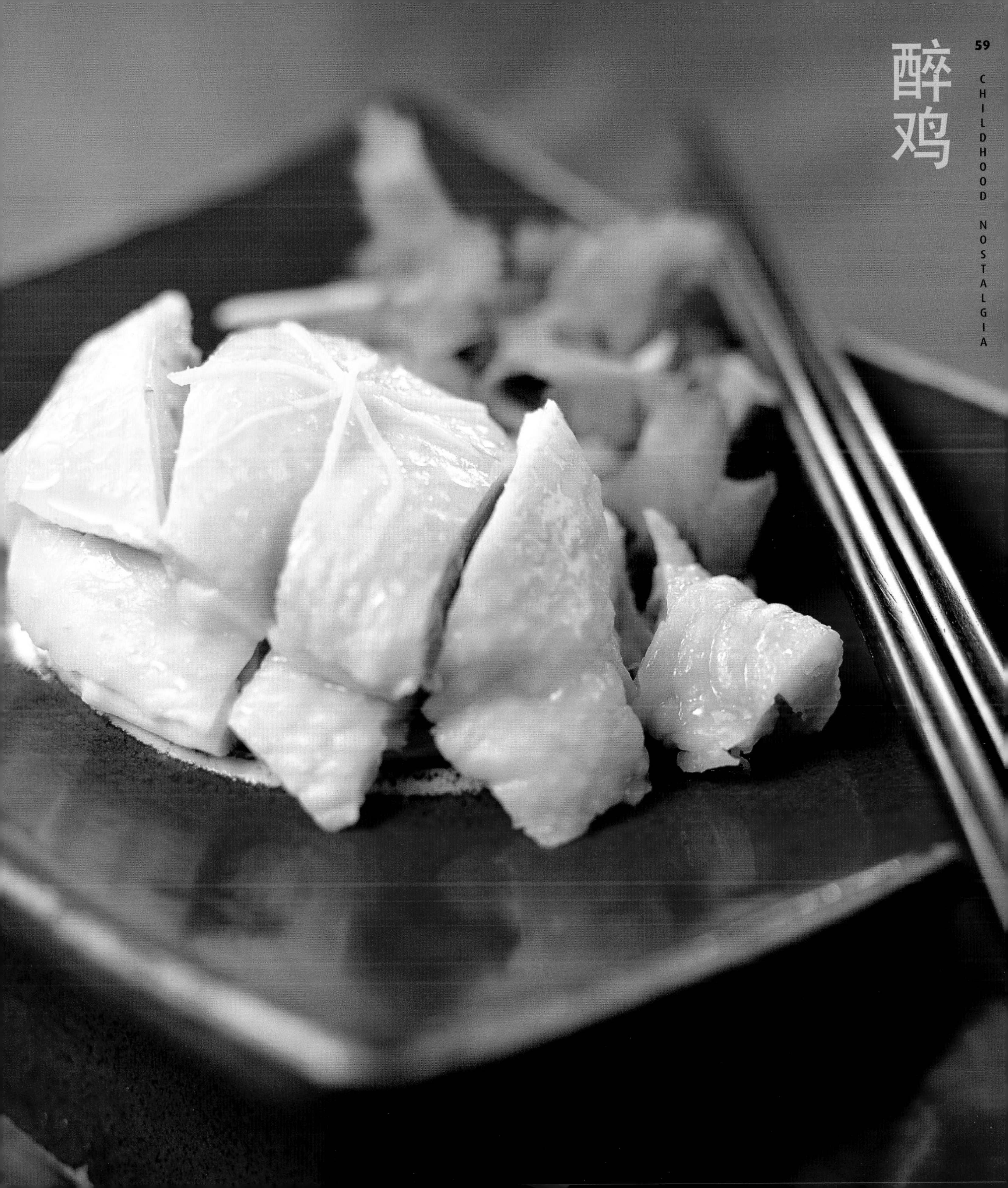

Kaofu with Mushroom and Black Fungus

INGREDIENTS

Kaofu
1 piece, cut into six pieces

Mushrooms
4 pieces, soaked in water till soft

Black fungus
4 pieces, soaked in water till soft

Cooking oil

Lily bulb
$^1/_2$ cup, soaked in water till soft

Carrots
$^1/_4$ cup, sliced (optional)

Spring onion
2 heads

Light soy sauce
to taste

Water or stock
$^1/_2$ cup

Salt
to taste

Sugar
to taste

METHOD

- Blanch kaofu in hot water for a few minutes. Squeeze completely dry and put aside.

- Remove mushrooms and black fungus from water. Squeeze dry, cut into bite-sized pieces and set aside.

- Heat enough oil in a wok and deep-fry the kaofu pieces till golden brown. Set aside.

- Heat 2 tsp of oil in a wok, and stir-fry the spring onion. Add kaofu, mushrooms, black fungus, lily bulb and carrots and stir-fry well.

- Add light soy sauce to taste. Add $^1/_2$ cup of water or stock, and cook for about 20 minutes till ingredients are soft.

- Add salt and sugar to taste before serving.

Smoked Grass Carp

INGREDIENTS

Grass carp
10 fillets, halved

Salt
$^1/_2$ tsp

Five-spice powder
$^1/_2$ tsp

Cornstarch
1 Tbsp

Cooking oil
2 cups

Seasoning:

Light soy sauce
1$^1/_2$ cups

Dark soy sauce
2 Tbsp

Rock sugar
$^1/_2$ cup

Cinnamon stick
2

Star anise
1

Garlic
1 clove

Ginger
2 slices

Hua Tiao wine
2 Tbsp

METHOD

• Rub fish fillets with salt and five-spice powder. Lightly coat with cornstarch.

• Mix the seasoning ingredients well and simmer for about 10 minutes or until the rock sugar fully dissolves. Set aside this marinade to cool.

• Heat 2 cups of oil and deep-fry fish until golden brown.

• Dip fish fillets completely in marinade.

• Serve hot or cold.

熏鱼

Yellow Croaker with Bamboo Shoot

INGREDIENTS

Yellow croaker
1

Salt
a pinch

Cornstarch
1 Tbsp

Chicken stock
1 cup

Ginger
6 slices

Spring onion
1 stalk

Cooking oil
2 Tbsp

Preserved vegetables
20g

Bamboo shoot
$1/4$ cup, cut into slices

Chinese ham
20g, steamed and cut into thin slices

Chinese wine
a dash

Pepper
a dash

METHOD

- Clean fish thoroughly and rub with a pinch of salt. Coat lightly with cornstarch.

- Boil chicken stock.

- Fry ginger and spring onion with 2 Tbsp oil until fragrant. Add fish and fry each side until golden brown.

- Add chicken stock and cook over a high heat for 5–10 minutes.

- Add preserved vegetables, bamboo shoot and Chinese ham and cook for another 5 minutes over medium heat.

- Drizzle with Chinese wine and bring to boil again.

- Remove and serve hot with a dash of pepper.

Potato Salad

INGREDIENTS

Potatoes
3, medium-sized

Salt
1 Tbsp

Carrot
1

Apples
2

Green peas
$^1/_2$ cup

Ham
50g, cut into cubes

Eggs
6, hard-boiled.
Separate yolks
and whites.

Coriander leaves
for garnish

Lettuce
for garnish

Dressing:

Mayonnaise
$^1/_2$ cup, non-fat

Tomato sauce
1 Tbsp

Lemon
1, juice

Tabasco sauce
to taste

METHOD

- Immerse potatoes in a large pot of water. Boil thoroughly.

- Remove the potatoes and immerse again in cold salted water. When cool, peel potatoes and cut into 1-cm cubes.

- Peel and boil carrot till cooked. Drain and cut into 1-cm cubes.

- Peel apples and dice into 1-cm cubes. Immerse in cold salted water.

- Blanch green peas in lightly salted boiling water for 5 minutes. Drain and rinse with cold water.

- Cut ham into 1-cm cubes.

- Chop egg whites into small pieces. Mash the egg yolks finely.

- Mix all ingredients in a big bowl, add dressing and chill.

- Serve cold, garnished with coriander leaves and lettuce.

洋山芋沙拉

Russian Borscht

INGREDIENTS

Beef shank
1 (about 1kg), chopped into pieces

Water
10 cups

Ginger
2 slices

Cooking oil
1 Tbsp

Onion
1, sliced thickly

Tomatoes
3, skinned and cut into chunks

Tomato paste
2 Tbsp

Carrots
2, cut into 1-cm cubes

Potatoes
3, skinned and cut into chunks

Cabbage
1, cut into large pieces

Salt
to taste

Pepper
to taste

Whipped cream

METHOD

- Blanch beef in boiling water for 10 minutes. Rinse under cold water and drain.

- Boil 10 cups of water, 2 slices of ginger and beef in a large saucepan over high heat. Lower heat when the water begins to boil and let simmer for approximately 1 hour or till beef turns tender.

- Heat 1 Tbsp of oil in a frying pan and stir-fry onion until soft. Add chopped tomatoes and stir-fry till soft. Add tomato paste and mix well.

- Add mixture, carrots and potatoes into simmering beef soup and continue to cook for 30–40 minutes.

- Add cabbage and simmer for another 15 minutes or until cabbage turns soft.

- Add salt and pepper to taste.

- Serve in individual bowls with a dollop of cream.

罗宋汤

My father was a musician; he played the 'erhu', a Chinese string instrument.

That elusive smile

When I was small, my father seemed to me someone stoic by nature and serious in demeanor, but he had a way of expressing his love for us— with food. Even when down to his last $10, he would spend it all on getting the best meal for us. I remember our dining table was a spread at every meal...and it was because of him.

My father loved seafood. In this respect, I was very much like him when I was young. My favourites were red-braised yellow fish, fried freshwater prawns and hairy crabs. I loved eating the skin off the red-braised yellow fish, and my father would always save it for me.

We both shared a love for fried freshwater prawns too. Fried with spring onions, ginger, soy sauce and sugar, the prawns glistened with a lovely red hue. I would often eat them whole—head, shell and all. It was simply divine. Everyone would have left the table, but I'd still be there, polishing off what was left of the prawns. Even when my lips bled, I couldn't stop myself eating. My father would sit across from me, watching me eat. It seemed to comfort him; at times a satisfied smile— which was rare—would spread across his lips. This is my most cherished childhood memory of my father and me.

Fried Freshwater Prawns

INGREDIENTS

Cooking oil
1 Tbsp

Ginger
3 slices

Spring onions
2 stalks

Freshwater prawns
500g, cleaned

Rice wine
1 Tbsp

Sauce:

Light soy sauce
1 1/2 Tbsp

Dark soy sauce
1 tsp

Sugar
2 tsp

Water
2 tsp

METHOD

- Heat 1 Tbsp of oil in a wok. Stir-fry ginger and 1 stalk spring onion until fragrant.

- Fry prawns until pink.

- Drizzle 1 Tbsp of wine over prawns and stir well.

- Add sauce and the remaining spring onion.

- Remove prawns to a serving dish and serve hot.

油爆虾

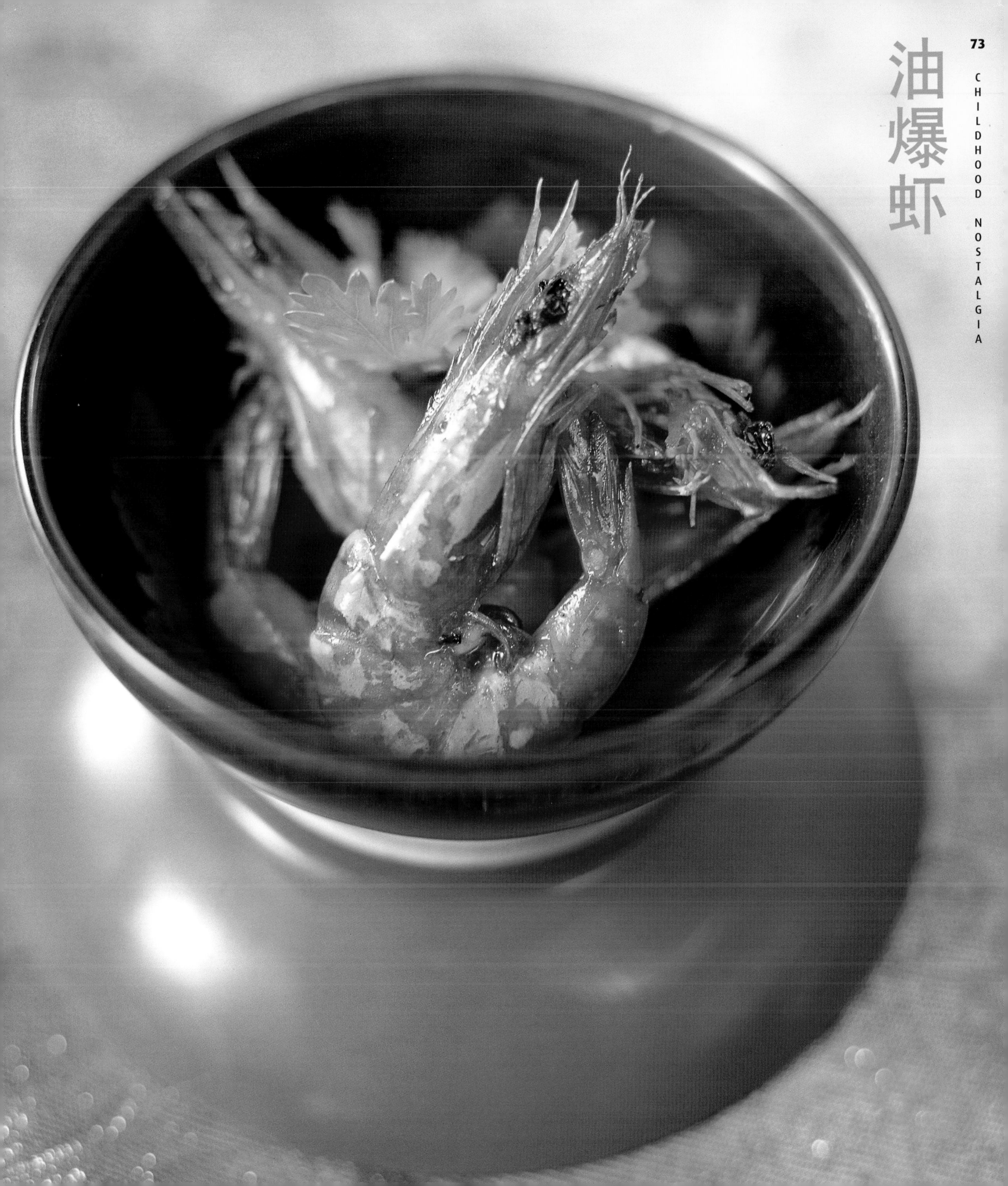

On an outing with dad and my two younger brothers at Victoria Park, Hong Kong.

Days of wine and odours

Fermented wine is a speciality of Shanghai. It is an intriguing mix of smells—the light sour-sweetness of wine and the dry fragrance of glutinous rice. On cold winter mornings during my childhood, my father would crack an egg into fermented wine and boil it. My mother said the blend was good for girls. In any case, whatever my father ate, I would always want a bite too.

Once I recall my father wrapping a huge glass container with a thick blanket, which he instructed us not to unwrap. He was in fact trying to make his own fermented wine at home. Whether the experiment succeeded I couldn't remember. But I do remember the sour-sweet smell that drifted through the house, and that strange blanket-covered jar sitting under the chair.

Apart from cracking an egg into the fermented wine, glutinous rice dumplings are a popular addition to the brew. Add in a little osmanthus and some diced tangerine, and you'd have a perfect after-meal dessert!

Sweet Fermented Glutinous Rice and Dumpling Dessert

INGREDIENTS

Glutinous rice flour
$^1/_2$ cup

Sugar
1 Tbsp

Hot water
2 cups

Rock sugar
$^1/_2$ cup

Dried osmanthus
1 tsp

Sweet fermented glutinous rice
6 Tbsp

Tangerine pulp
$^1/_4$ piece, thinly shredded

METHOD

• Mix glutinous rice flour and sugar in a big bowl. Add hot water, a little at a time and mix to a dough. Knead the dough until smooth. Divide the dough into several portions. Roll each portion into a long strip about 1.5 cm in diameter. Cut the strip into 1-cm lengths and roll each piece into a tiny ball with your palms. Set aside and cover with a wet towel.

• Boil 2 cups of water with $^1/_2$ cup rock sugar until the sugar dissolves.

• Add the dumplings and cook for 3–5 minutes. Add 1 tsp of dried osmanthus and cook for 2 minutes. Turn off the heat.

• Add sweet fermented glutinous rice. Serve in individual bowls garnished with tangerine pulp.

酒酿丸子

Soda bubbles—a farewell to childhood

On hot summer evenings after dinner, my grandma would give us kids some money, and that would signal the start of the most eagerly anticipated event of the week for us.

We'd race to the store and back with the ice cream—always a box of Neapolitan with its layers of colour: white, pink and brown, I remember. Then all eyes would be on grandma for the all-important distribution of the ice cream. As the cut slices fell, the slightest difference we thought we saw in the size of the portions would draw immediate howls of protest. And while my brothers might be content with just one or two colours, I would insist on having all three, because they were the brightest, most beautiful colours I had ever seen.

I had to have them all.

Then, carrying my tri-coloured treasure in a cup, I would get the soda. I'd pour it, hissing and cascading down over the ice cream. My nostrils would catch the faint whiff of vanilla—sweet and slightly artificial—as the colours drowned in the froth of a thousand bubbles. Then it was a race against time, scooping the delicious gooey lumps of cream into my mouth as quickly as possible, before they melted into a thick, colour-streaked mixture. Spoonful after spoonful...

It is clear as daylight even today—the smells, the colours, the saccharine flavours, the feel of the cold goo sliding down my throat. When I recall my childhood, this is always what I see; but it is wraith-like, as all memory is, and disappears into nothingness as quickly as the froth in my soda.

Sandy's faces behind the flavours

Let's face it!

My past will always be a cherished part of me but life, like a cuisine, continues to unfold; and each day brings its own surprises.

Zoom to the present—to Shanghai, a city redolent with memories for me, yet whose face is turned to a dazzling culinary future. It is here that my food journey continues.

When it comes to the kitchen, my dreams have always outstripped my ability. All my labours at the frying pan and wok have only served to make me more painfully aware of how much I need to learn. The recipes in the earlier pages, though close to my heart, are after all, products of a humble family kitchen.

The opportunity to do this book has therefore been a godsend. It's opened doors for me to some of the finest culinary talents and restaurateurs in Shanghai—and allowed me to unashamedly tap their brains without having to pay a cent in tuition fees!

Just a face in the crowd

Behind every great dish is a great chef, but how often, when we enjoy a great meal at a restaurant, do we think of the person behind it? Well, speaking to these chefs and restaurateurs has allowed me to put a human face to the recipes and eating establishments you'll see in the book. And what a face it is!

The vision, passion and dedication of these people are amazing. Food and cooking—and the quest for culinary perfection—are literally their

lives. Whatever their clientele, and whatever their culinary tradition and style, they make up the true face of Shanghai cuisine today. They are the reason why 'foodies' and gourmets flock to Shanghai in droves, and why the Shanghainese-in-the-street eats so inexpensively—yet so well—each and every day.

Food face!

Take Chef Jereme Leung, for instance, whose ceaseless and creative explorations of the boundaries of old and new, East and West have resulted in bold recipes such as his Sugar-cured Glutinous Red Dates with Foie Gras. Or Chef Qian Shixian, who makes working look so light and easy. His seemingly effortless creation of ethereal masterpieces such as his rose-petal prawns belie the amount of thought and work—and heart—that went into it.

Other chefs appear founts of experience and wisdom; take Uncle Li of Shanghai Uncle, who lives up to his avuncular nickname in every sense. Uncle Li good-naturedly dispenses insights into life and living along with nuggets of advice on cooking. As I get on in years myself, I begin to truly appreciate the value of such conversations—as I did the wonderful meeting I had with Chef Susumu Fukui of La Villa Rouge. Chef Fukui's enthusiasm for his art, his earnest striving to learn, and openness about the goals and desires of his life, I found especially touching.

Then through Paul Hsu, a restaurateur, I was offered a glimpse of the other face of dining in Shanghai—a face no less fascinating, and peopled by visionaries with similar passions and drive.

Paul's fascinating tales of his experiences in the far reaches of China in search of quality—both of talent and ingredients—will, in time, I'm sure, become the stuff of culinary legends in Shanghai. I've come to see that people like Paul and his restaurant, Ye Shanghai, act as the bedrock of stability for Shanghainese chefs, and the catalyst that spurs them to hone their skills and scale the heights of their profession.

A full-face view

I came to the interviews hoping to glean a few tips here and there on sharpening my kitchen skills (and to taste some great food along the way!) but got far, far more than I bargained for. I've met some of the most interesting—and nicest—people in my life, and saw for a moment, however sketchily, the breathtaking face of professional cooking and food entertainment in Shanghai.

It has been more than a privilege—it's been an inspiration.

Ah Niang

TAIHE YINSHI DIAN
19 Sinan Lu

O N this street, Ah Niang calls the shots.

The diners at her shop double-park along the street
with impunity. Her tables spill onto the sidewalk, when
they shouldn't. Ah Niang not only gets away with
these, she's one of the most well-loved and respected
figures on this street. No cop would dream of giving
this grandma a ticket!

**With Ah Niang in front
of her shop.**

The shop may be named Taihe, but everyone in this city knows it as Ah Niang Mee Gu, or Mum's noodle shop.

Beginning as a tiny shop-front business, Ah Niang now commands another shop across the street; it's her extended dining unit, holding just seats and tables.

The 72-year-old matriarch, who used to teach kindergarten, believes in doing some things the way they have always been done—like washing preserved vegetables in the ancient sink by the walkway just outside the shop before dicing them, and selling her salted vegetables and meat noodles at 4 yuan, the deep-fried eel noodles at 8 yuan and the yellow fish noodles at 12 yuan— the same prices as when she first opened twelve years ago!

These days, the noodle shop draws not just Shanghai residents but food critics as well, and Ah Niang is something of a celebrity, having been featured in many a food guide and review.

Ah Niang makes her own preserved vegetables (top) and fries them with shredded pork (bottom).

However, Ah Niang wears her fame lightly—this somewhat portly figure in a plaid green cardigan.

Also, make no mistake; this spunky lady has an unbelievable tale to tell. The secret of her success apparently lies in the mysterious stock which goes into the soup. This tantalising mixture was the jealously-guarded secret of a chef Ah Niang hired when she first started. The chef told no one—not even Ah Niang herself.

So every morning, as the chef prepared his recipe, Ah Niang would peep at him from upstairs through a hole in the floorboards, and she soon uncovered his secret. A secret she hopes someday to bequeath to her only grandson, a student in Vancouver.

But for now, the sole guardian of the secret recipe continues to wake at three every morning to prepare the stock. "It's all non-meat ingredients" was all she divulged. Ah Niang serves her first bowl at 6.30am and by 1.30pm—and 500 bowls of noodles later—she closes her shop.

Ah Niang hasn't forgotten her unwitting benefactor though; every month she gives the chef an allowance.

"I'm someone who's sentimental and I don't forget people who have helped me."

Prices frozen in time (top); a waitress dishes out the goodies (bottom left); and a satisfied customer (bottom right).

"Every day is like my birthday, because I eat noodles every day."

– Ah Niang

Ah Niang & my two grandmas

What grandma said to me

In Ningbo dialect, Ah Niang means grandmother. I like the way 'Ah Niang' sounds; it has a homely, comforting ring to it—the way I always thought a grandmother ought to be. I remember well my maternal grandma. She once said to me, "When you've made it and have earned lots of money, then I'll take your allowance." I had offered her a stipend at a time when I was making peanuts on my first job. She never accepted it.

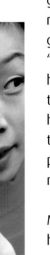

My dad's mother, on the other hand, I never met. To me, she was hardly more than a face in old family photos. However, I do remember that I was ten when she died. It was a cloudy and gray winter afternoon, and I can still clearly see my father sitting in a dark room, grieving. It was the first time I saw him cry.

We visited Ah Niang on a sunny afternoon, and gently awoke her from her nap. She brought us from across the street, where she lived, to her little shop, smoothing her tousled hair with her hands as we went along. I spoke to the old lady of my love for shredded pork and snow cabbage noodles, and asked if she could make me a bowl.

Noodles on the streetside

She promptly set her young kitchen help to dicing the snow cabbage—"No ends. Just take the centre, which is the best part." The stove was fired up and the diced vegetables, along with other ingredients, brought in.

Ah Niang laced the wok with oil, and spooned in the sugar with the vegetables and shredded meat. I paused a moment, anxious about the wanton helpings of oil and sugar. But the aroma rising from the wok quickly ended any such hesitation with a flourish, and I was soon helping to cart steaming bowls of noodles to the table. We downed bowl after bowl, our crew of ten and myself. And Ah Niang herself wasn't holding back; crab noodles, yellow fish noodles and my favourite, noodles with shredded pork and snow cabbage—they were all there and they tasted incredible.

When we rose to pay for the meal, Ah Niang refused to accept a cent. She said to me in Ningbo, "When your book is published and has made lots of money, come back and visit me."

My maternal grandma's words echoed through my mind at that moment. I thought of her and my other grandma, whose voice I never heard, but which I was sure, would have been just as gentle and loving. My tears welled up.

Table talk

Sandy:
Your noodles are well known for the stock. How did you learn to make it?

Ah Niang:
When I first started, I hired a chef from Can Lang Ting (a Shanghai noodle institution) who was very secretive about what he put into the stock. So I would wake up at 2:30 every morning and look through a peephole while he prepared the stock for the day. That's how I knew what went into his stock so that when he fell ill, I was ready to take over.

Sandy:
Why haven't you raised your prices all these twelve years?

Ah Niang:
I'm not like most young people these days. I'm not interested in making lots of money. All I want is for people to come here and eat often, and be happy. I like crowds.

Chef Jereme Leung

WHAMPOA CLUB, THREE ON THE BUND
5, The Bund, Zhongshan Dongyi Lu

W ith his no-nonsense buzz cut and compact, energetic frame, Chef Jereme Leung looks every inch the man on a mission—one that seeks to re-invent Shanghainese cuisine.

Sandy learns from the master himself, Chef Jereme Leung (right), the finer points of rolling crabmeat 'tong yuen' or rice dumplings (top).

By 'presenting the best of the past, present and future of this wonderful Chinese heritage', the chef is intent on setting the epicentre of the Shanghai culinary scene on his brand-new, and very exclusive, restaurant on the Bund, Whampoa Club. Sounds like hard work? Chef Leung is no stranger to that.

From his career-start as a kitchen help in Hong Kong at age 13, Chef Leung has become an internationally acclaimed chef heading one of the premier Chinese restaurants of Shanghai—if not China. On his way up, his professional highs include his appointment as Executive Chef at Jiang-Nan Chun, Four Seasons Hotel's flagship restaurant in Singapore, and being numbered among the 'World's Best Chefs' in 2000 by The American Academy of Hospitality Science—an accolade shared with other culinary luminaries such as Charles Trotter, Jean-George Vongerichten and Wolfgang Puck.

Despite such a resume—and the self-assurance that comes with it—the Hong Kong-born, Singapore-bred chef concedes his task would be a challenge. But it's a challenge he relishes. Speaking as a non-native 'outsider', he thinks Shanghai is a culinary capital-in-waiting—it has the makings but is not quite ready yet.

Two things stand in its way: the difficulty of getting exclusive ingredients and an inadequate training infrastructure for personnel in the industry. The city's increasingly competitive dining scene and its search for international culinary recognition make these concerns pressing, and he feels they should be addressed.

Kneading the dough for the 'tong yuen' (opposite page) and boiling the rice dumplings in hot water (bottom).

But it's in another area that the chef feels he can make a difference.

He tells me that Shanghainese cuisine, being the youngest of eight major regional cuisines of China, draws from many older sources and influences. But it has, so to speak, fallen on hard times—losing some of its traditions and recipes in the wake of the political instability of the thirties, and the Cultural Revolution which followed.

Chef Leung hopes to recoup those losses and revitalise the cuisine. He thinks he has made significant headway. For instance, do you know what's behind that beautifully bright red glaze that coats Shanghai's famous red-braised dishes, like the red-braised fish tail? Chef Leung's answer: they apply a cooking method that melts large amounts of sugar in warm oil.

The rediscovery of lost traditions and cooking secrets like these has led to the resurrection of old favourites like the famous Shanghai drunken crab. But while the traditional recipe calls for the use of wine with a quite intoxicating alcohol content, Chef Leung's reinterpretation tempers the wine, and washes the crab in an exquisitely subtle vinegar-tinged stock. It is re-invention at its best.

So while the unqualified success of Whampoa Club is the man's immediate goal, the chef knows he can do that *and* take Shanghai cuisine to a 'new level, both in food and service standards'.

The delicate skills required of the 'tong yuen' maker.

"I believe that the key to excellent Chinese cooking lies not just in knowing how food is prepared, but in having a deep understanding of the characteristics of different foods and their origins, as well as the use of ingredients in various cuisines and cultures."

– Chef Jereme Leung

Table talk

Sandy:
What's your philosophy when it comes to food and cooking?

Chef Leung:
No cook is better than his ingredients. And whichever cuisine one specialises in, it is most important to get the basics right before you embark on creating or recreating a cuisine. 'Fusion' may become 'confusion' when cooks do not know this important and basic principle.

Sandy:
How do you sustain creativity? What inspires you?

Chef Leung:
I read a lot; I keep updated by continually reading wine and food publications, and by collecting cookbooks—I have more than a thousand of them in my library at home. I learn a lot by reading about other culinary professionals, especially their thoughts and unique takes on their particular cuisines. Travelling has also greatly influenced my life and my perceptions of food.

And finally, there are food promotions, which I have conducted in various countries over the years. Through them, I've met many different people and observed all sorts of cooking styles, and this has certainly opened my mind to new possibilities too.

Hairy Crab Glutinous Rice Dumplings

INGREDIENTS

Minced crabmeat
30g

Glutinous rice flour
30g

Wheat starch
7.5g

Vegetable shortening
5g

Chinese choi sum
1 stalk

Seasoning:

Ginger
10g

Onion infused oil*
20ml

Chicken stock
150ml

Hua Diao wine
10ml

Salt
$1/4$ tsp

Sugar
$1/4$ tsp

Pepper
to taste

Potato starch
1 tsp

Water
20ml

METHOD

- Stir-fry the ginger with the infused oil till fragrant. Add the minced crabmeat, chicken stock, 10ml of wine, a pinch of salt, a pinch of sugar and pepper to taste. Add potato starch and stir-fry until the mixture thickens slightly. Turn off the heat and allow to cool. Shape into small balls and store in chiller.

- Knead the glutinous rice flour with 20ml of water. Boil the wheat starch and sugar in 5ml of water. Add it to the glutinous dough with 5g vegetable shortening and knead into a smooth dough. Then, take a small portion and fill with minced crabmeat. Shape it into a small dumpling. Continue with the rest of the glutinous dough and minced crabmeat.

- Bring 2 cups of water to the boil. Add the dumplings and cook till dumplings float. Drain and transfer dumplings to a serving soup bowl.

- Boil the chicken stock and season with a few drops of wine, a pinch of salt and a pinch of sugar. Add the Chinese choi sum and pour soup and vegetable into the serving bowl with dumplings. Serve immediately.

* To prepare onion infused oil, fry an onion or shallot in oil. Remove the onion or shallot when it turns brown.

Drunken Crab

INGREDIENTS

Fresh hairy crabs
465g

Seasoning:

Chicken stock
125ml

Sugar
96g

Kikkoman soy sauce
62.5ml

Dark soy sauce
1 tsp

Changjiang vinegar
100ml

Zhengjiang vinegar
100ml

Ginger
50g, shredded

METHOD

- Make a cut through the middle of the crab and wash the crab, removing its internal organs. Make two cuts on the small joints of each crab leg. Remove the claws and break them with the back of a cleaver to loosen the meat.

- Put the seasoning in a pot (except vinegar and ginger) and bring to a boil. Allow to cool.

- Add the Changjiang vinegar and Zhengjiang vinegar.

- Stir-fry the ginger till fragrant, then add to the marinade in the pot. Put in the crabs and leave to soak for at least 8 hours in the chiller. Serve cold with some marinade as desired.

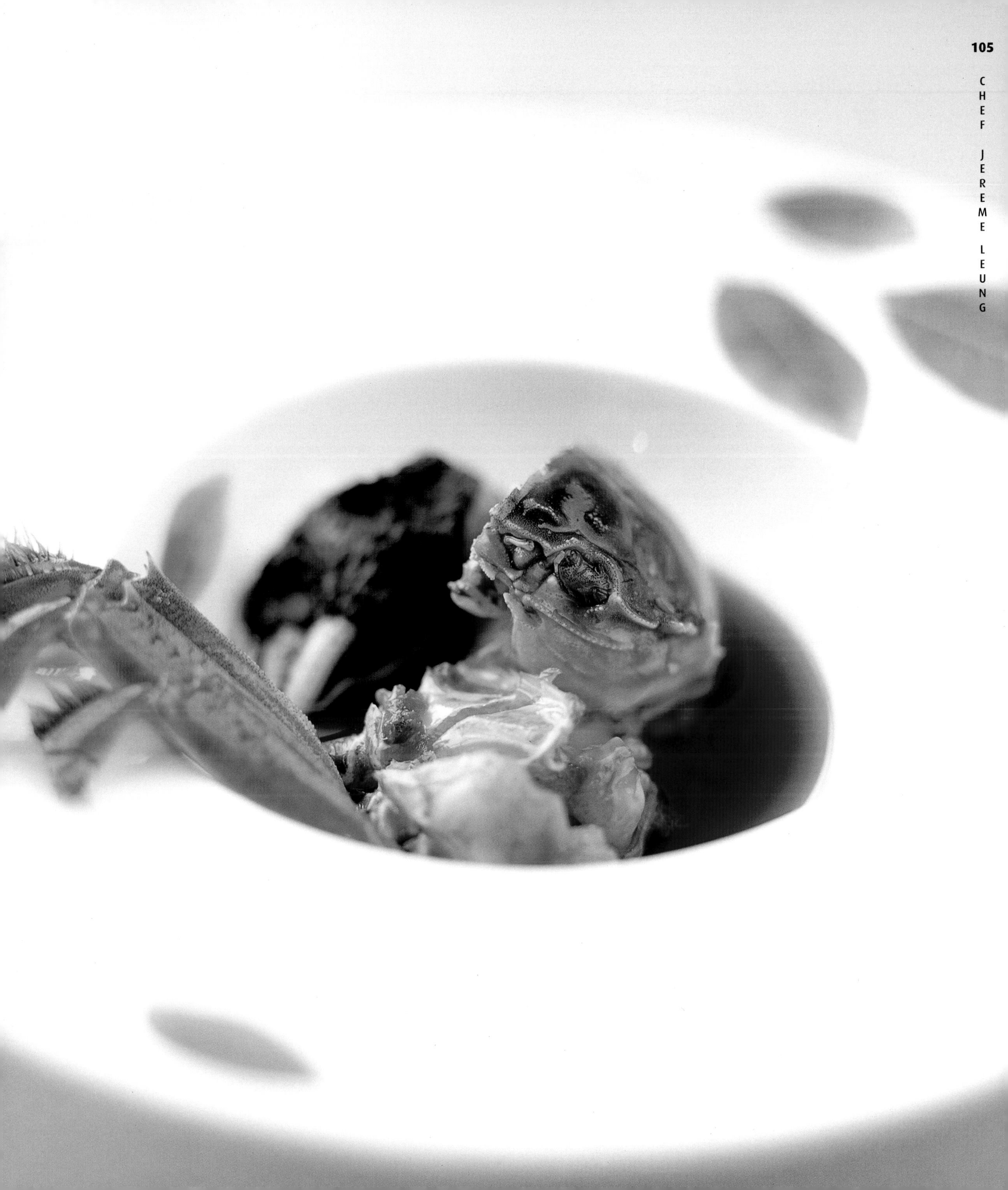

Sugar-cured Glutinous Red Dates with Foie Gras

INGREDIENTS

Chinese red dates
12

Glutinous rice flour
30g

Water
30ml

Wheat starch
7.5g

Sugar
7g

Vegetable shortening
5g

Foie Gras (goose liver)
200g

Celery
15g

Lily bulb
15g

Apples, diced
30g

Seasoning:

Sugar
30g

Light syrup*
250ml, steamed

Salt
2g

Garlic
10g, chopped

Shallots
10g, sliced

Coriander
10g

Coarse black pepper
$^1/_4$ tsp

Virgin olive oil
30ml

Cinnamon powder
a dash

Ginger
30g, shredded, for garnish

METHOD

- Clean the red dates, remove the core and mix evenly with 20g of sugar. Steam for 30 min. Remove and set aside.

- Knead the glutinous rice flour with 25ml of water. Boil 5ml water and 7g of sugar with the wheat starch and add to the glutinous dough with 5g vegetable shortening. Knead into a smooth dough.

- Fill the red dates with the glutinous dough. Add the dates to 250ml of light syrup and steam for another 3 min.

- Mix the salt, garlic, shallots, coriander, coarse black pepper and virgin olive oil well. Add the foie gras into the mix and pan-fry it till slightly golden.

- Slice the celery into diamond shapes, then scald and drain. Slice the lily bulb thickly. Mix the two ingredients together.

- Fry the diced apples with oil and a little water; add sugar and cinnamon powder to taste and continue to fry until the apples turn soft.

- Place the celery and lily bulb mixture on a plate and add, in this order, the red dates, diced apples, foie gras, light syrup and decorate with fried threadlike ginger and shallot tips.

- Serve immediately as a cold starter.

* To make light syrup, boil 100ml water with 200g sugar until the sugar dissolves.

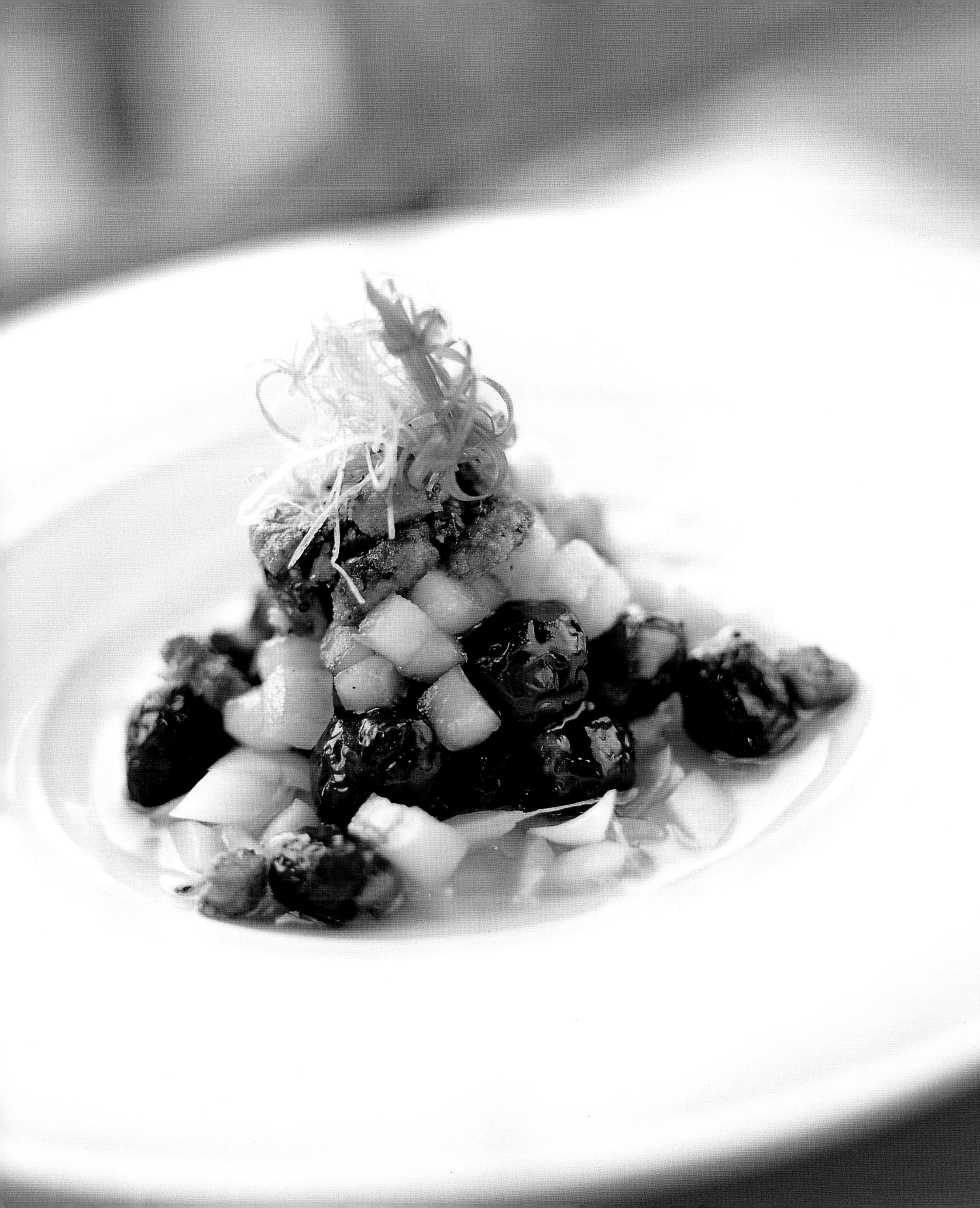

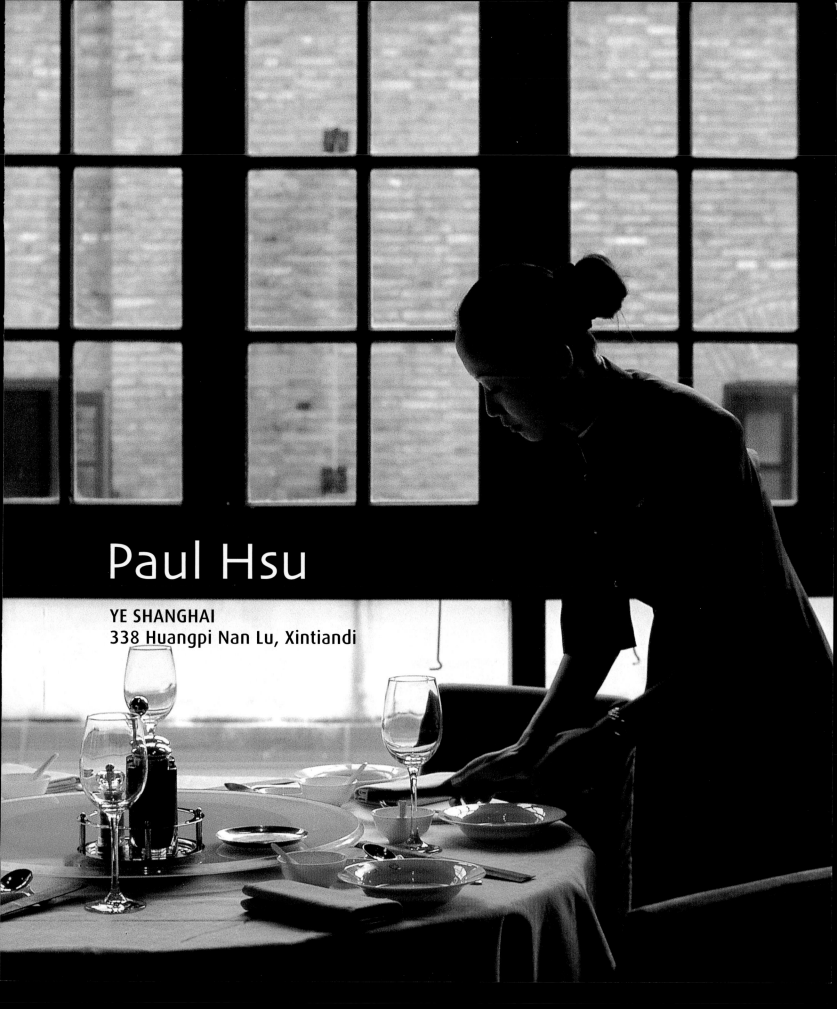

Paul Hsu

YE SHANGHAI
338 Huangpi Nan Lu, Xintiandi

A Hong Kong-born, Cornell-educated restaurateur holds forth on the intricacies of traditional Shanghainese cuisine in a restaurant that is a Western-concocted dream of a Chinese interior.

Chinese tea re-invented (top); the chinois chic elegance of Ye Shanghai (right).

Is it for real?

You'd better believe it.

The place is Ye Shanghai and the man is Paul Hsu, and if you're anybody who's somebody in the hip Shanghai food-and-glamour scene, this is where you want to be.

Ye Shanghai is located in the Xintiandi neighbourhood. This is Shanghai's *numero uno* food and entertainment enclave, where French Concession architecture—the most characteristic of which is the shikumen or stone gate house—creates a rusticated, period ambience.

Shops, restaurants and bars occupy many of these historic buildings—as does Ye Shanghai. What sets it apart, however, is its chinois chic décor and its regular champagne parties, which draw the hip and the expatriate crowds. Both are the brainchildren of Paul Hsu, who insists "there's nothing wrong with looking good". We couldn't

agree with him more—provided it comes with good food.

No fear about this though.

While at first sight, Paul's credentials might be incongruous with the culinary tradition he espouses (he jokes that he speaks Shanghainese only 'after a few drinks'), they are rock solid—and he knows his food. Of Shanghainese parentage, Paul's a graduate of Cornell University's School of Hotel Administration. He cut his professional teeth in Hong Kong, where he introduced—apart from Modern Shanghainese—Retro Vietnamese, Rustic Italian, French Provencal and Modern Japanese to its fine dining scene.

Without a doubt, with Paul at the helm, Ye Shanghai is fabulous to look at—and eat at. And while his culinary focus might be thought of as provincial—the perfection of Shanghainese cuisine, the search for better ingredients and healthier ways of cooking—his business mind thinks global.

He dreams of bringing Shanghai to the world; he plans to open in Tokyo and Paris next, and have eight restaurants in eight different cities across the world. It'll require talent, he says, and that will come from Shanghai.

Isn't it a wonderful thing, I thought, that we now have the means to take great recipes and cooking thousands of miles from their places of origin, to food lovers around the world for them to appreciate and enjoy?

As with Ye Shanghai, this will definitely be more than a dream. We wish Paul the best.

Passion and concentration in front of the wok. Each chef has his own specific duty and speciality.

Table talk

Sandy:
Would you consider the food here authentic Shanghainese?

Paul:
I think it's authentic to its roots; but the taste is different from, say, a local eatery, where they might serve the same dish but it's geared to the local Shanghainese taste—much sweeter, stronger and heavier flavours. Here, the international clientele are more conscious of their health, so we adjust. I don't think we're paring down the taste, we're simply striking a balance.

Sandy:
I notice that not all the chefs are from Shanghai...

Paul:
You're right, they're not all from Shanghai. It's better this way— they can share their different ideas about food, and they also learn faster because they're more competitive. We call them our kids.

Sandy:
I remember certain dishes I enjoyed as a child. They don't taste the same anymore when I eat them today. Why is that?

Paul:
Most chefs will tell you it's a matter of consistency. In Hong Kong, for example, it's up to the chef to decide how much or how little to put in. That's why here, we learn to be more consistent. It's a challenge, you know, to get every chef to produce the same high standards.

It helps when you keep the flavours simple and not too complicated. Try to keep it, for instance, within three different flavours. That way, people are able to taste what they eat. Here at the restaurant, we spend more time now on our ingredients, on sourcing them and working with higher quality ingredients. Sadly, when it comes to this, the Chinese are still not as sophisticated as the Westerners.

"**They said I was crazy to open a Shanghainese restaurant in Shanghai. But what we offer is a complete dining experience—the ambience, service, location, history. It's not just about the food...not all Chinese appreciate this.**"

– Paul Hsu

Snow Cabbage with Green Soy Beans and Beancurd Sheets

INGREDIENTS

Hangzhou beancurd sheet
150g

Snow cabbage
50g

Green soy beans
50g

Lard
1 Tbsp

Seasoning:

Clear soup or chicken broth
$^1/_4$ cup

Salt
7.5g

Msg
5g

Chicken essence powder
5g

Millet or rice wine
1 Tbsp

Pepper
to taste

METHOD

- Slice the beancurd sheets into pieces, $^1/_2$-inch wide and 1-inch long.

- Dice the stem of the snow cabbage.

- Put the beancurd sheets and soy beans in boiling water.

- Heat lard in a wok and stir-fry the diced snow cabbage till fragrant.

- Add clear soup, beancurd sheets and soy beans and bring to boil.

- Add seasoning before serving.

Stir-fried Rice Cake with Bean Paste

INGREDIENTS

Rice cake
150g

Fried diced chicken
50g

Green soy beans
50g

Seasoning:

Ginger
2 slices

Spring onions
2 stalks, sliced

Sweet black bean sauce
100ml

Chicken essence powder
5g

Dark soy sauce
50ml

Sugar
50g

Msg
10g

Rice wine
1 Tbsp

Pepper
to taste

METHOD

- Cook the rice cake, diced chicken and soy beans in boiling water. Drain and set aside.

- Heat the wok and fry some ginger slices and spring onions till fragrant. Add sweet black bean sauce.

- Add the chicken essence powder and the cooked ingredients and simmer for 20 min. Add dark soy sauce, sugar and msg.

- Fry slowly till dry. Add wine and pepper and serve immediately.

Winter Bamboo Shoots, Salted Pork and Beancurd Soup

INGREDIENTS

Pork belly
100g

Salted pork
100g

Chilled winter bamboo shoots
50g, thinly sliced

Beancurd sheet
50g sliced into strips

Monkey head truffles
50g

Seasoning:

Spring onions,
1 stalk, sliced thickly

Lard
$1/2$ Tbsp

Clear soup or chicken broth
$1/4$ cup

Ginger
2 slices

Salt
10g

Msg
5g

Rice wine
1 Tbsp

Pepper
to taste

METHOD

- Cut pork belly into $1/2$-inch pieces and salted pork into $1/2$-inch strips.

- Cook all the ingredients in boiling water.

- Fry spring onions in lard till fragrant and add to clear soup together with some ginger slices and the cooked ingredients.

- Increase the heat and bring to a boil, then let simmer on medium heat.

- Add salt, msg, wine and pepper just before serving.

Mdm He Shuiying

JIAJIA TANG BAO DIAN
638 Henan Nan Lu

X

ianzuo, xianmai, xianzheng, xianchi (wrapped, steamed, sold, eaten ala minute). The sign outside the shop clearly gives notice that the customer is in for something different— this one has attitude...

Eating at Jiajia's is as much about the experience as the food.

The steam, hiss and bustle at the front of the shop.

佳家汤包

(现做、现卖、现蒸、现吃)

每笼一两半15只

纯鲜肉汤包　5.00

(早市供应,售完为止,恕不拆零)

虾仁鲜肉汤包 6.00

鸡丁鲜肉汤包 6.00

纯虾仁汤包　8.10

纯鸡丁汤包　7.20

蟹粉鲜肉汤包 15.00

纯蟹粉汤包　81.00

汤

鸡鸭血汤 每碗2.00

紫菜蛋皮汤 每碗2.00

生姜丝　　每碗1.00

外菜与酒谢绝入内

Steaming containers of dumplings (left); busy hands at the dumpling-making table (top).

This is Shanghai seen without rose-tinted glasses. For even as you wait in the ever-present queue outside the dilapidated doorway, you are assailed by the rising heat and steam and muffled hiss from the steamers that spill out to the sidewalk. When you notice the shop, what amaze you are its tiny proportions, and the amount of frenetic activity it seems to contain.

The shop is built several steps below the street, making it feel like you're eating in a pit. Around the few tables, which fill almost the entire space, six or seven girls circulate at speed, preparing the food and attending to the demands of twenty or so gesticulating diners huddled on stools and cramped elbow-to-elbow between the tables. And above the din, the ceiling fans whirl so low that they threaten to lob a finger or two off any over-enthusiastic guest waving for the attention of a waitress. Discomfort doesn't nearly describe it all.

Presently, the object of all the fuss arrives, in large steaming bamboo containers—the famous soup dumplings! Biting through the fabric-like veil of flour, the steaming contents fill your mouth—soupy, flavourful, satiating. Absolutely wonderful!

The shop is still very much a local 'secret' but word has got out, and foreign faces at the tables are increasingly common. Madam He Shuiying has owned the business for 20 years, and not once has she counted her shop's output of dumplings in a day. However, she reckons that she sells 70 kati (84 kilograms) of fresh pork a day, seven days a week. She opens at six in the morning, and says the meat usually runs out by five in the evening, when she closes. On weekends, the meat runs out by three in the afternoon. Her pork dumplings cost 5 yuan for fifteen, while the most expensive—the crab roe dumplings—cost 81 yuan.

Today, the queues for her dumplings are such that Madam He and her husband Mr Shen Dingyong, have introduced frozen dumplings for takeaway. Times are undeniably good these days, but the couple remember the circumstances that led to their hard-won success.

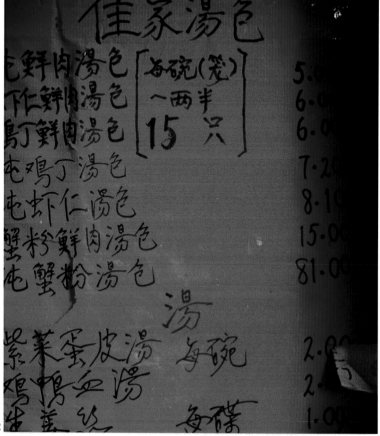

Their first business—selling noodles, buns and wontons—made them just one of thousands of other 'mom and pop' shops that fill Shanghai's streets. They were struggling and spent nights, after they had closed, thinking how to pick up the business. Steamed dumplings somehow became their solution.

They sampled as many dumplings as they could find in the city, then experimented and refined and finally developed their own. The rest, so the saying goes, is history.

Mr Shen and Madam He are now in semi-retirement. Their 27-year-old daughter runs Jiajia Tang Bao Dian, and if the shop sign and the ever-lengthening queues are any indication, she has certainly inherited her parents' genes for can-do attitude and sheer hard work.

Empty containers attest to the brisk business (opposite page: top); a scrawled promise of culinary heaven (opposite page: bottom); the dumplings are eaten with light vinegar and slivers of ginger (this page).

"You have to eat the crab roe dumpling piping hot and fresh from the steamer. Then you can taste the sweetness of it. Even one or two seconds later, and it doesn't taste as good anymore."

– Madam He

Table talk

Sandy:
People say that most chefs don't enjoy eating their own cooking. Do you eat your own dumplings?

Madam He:
I don't eat them, but it's because I don't like meat. However, my daughter grew up eating them.

Sandy:
How are your dumplings different from others?

Madam He:
We wrap our dumplings differently. While most dumplings receive a twist on top, we simply give ours a light pinch so that when they're steamed, the skin on top wouldn't be too hard.'

Chef Susumu Fukui

LA VILLA ROUGE
811 Hengshan Lu, Xu Jia Hui Park

A S dramatically as the city melds diverse cultures, so just as precociously does Chef Susumu Fukui straddle the great cuisines.

Chef Fukui calls what he does 'New Shanghai Cuisine', and what it is, is a seamless, inspired harmony of three great cuisines, Chinese, French and Japanese. There is a thread of creative energy running through the Shanghai culinary scene today that is Franco-Japanese fusion, and Chef Fukui is one of its pioneers.

He undoubtedly has the credentials for the status.

Trained in traditional French cooking, his resumé includes star billing at Fontainebleau at the Tokyo Imperial Hotel, La Petite Chaya and Symphonie in Los Angeles, Antica Osteria del Teatro in Piacenza, Italy and Sprendido at The Ritz-Carlton, Osaka.

And now Chef Fukui is at La Villa Rouge, which has the most expensive tables in Shanghai. He tells me that, being with the city and its food traditions for only a year, he's still on the learning curve as far as Chinese cuisine goes.

But already, ingredients such as broad bean paste, Chinese rice wine, jasmine tea and Peking duck are on his grocery list.

The conserved ambience of La Villa Rouge's historic interior (opposite page and this page).

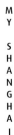

These things—together with other typically Western and Japanese ingredients—go into his signature dishes like Shanghainese Crab, Avocado Celeriac Timbale Salad with Aromatic Balsamic Sauce, Sauteed Australian Kobe Wagyu Beef and Assorted Mushrooms with Soy Cappuccino Sauce, Slowly Roasted Lamb Rack with Mixed Fresh Herbs and Potato with Black Pepper Sauce and Steamed Fresh Fish and Shellfish with Sea Urchin Sauce. It's clear the chef's sense of culinary fusion is fully up and running; he's just honing it to laser-sharp precision.

And that's really the icing on the cake to the La Villa Rouge dining experience. The clientele, which includes diplomats, top businessmen and movie stars, is here for the food, ambience, and a piece of history...in that order, I'm told. The restaurant occupies a French-colonial three-storey house which was a French recording studio, Pathe-Phone-Cinema-Chine, in the 1920s, then later in the 1930s, a recording studio for EMI. The Chinese national anthem was first performed here, and singers and songwriters such as Zhou Xuan, Xian Xinghai, Nie Er, Bai Guang and Li Jinguang have recorded here.

Slices of red radish (left); clarifying some finer points of cooking at La Villa Rouge's kitchen (opposite page).

"French, Chinese and Japanese are among the great cuisines. The fire and the Japanese know about good ingredients. If we can

French know about good sauces, the Chinese know how to use the harmonise the three—perfection."
– Chef Susumu Fukui

Table talk

Sandy:
The restaurant sits in a building with an important historical past. Has this in any way shaped your cooking?

Chef Fukui:
A restaurant should be evaluated as a 'total package', taking into consideration its location and ambience as well. I'm fortunate to have my food served in a building steeped in history. I must always be conscious not to betray the expectations of the people who come here to dine.

Sandy:
What is good fusion food?

Chef Fukui:
Good fusion is far from just a mishmash of different tastes; it requires a deep understanding of the traditions of each culture. One has to be committed to learning as much as possible about these traditions.

Sandy:
What do you hope to achieve and what do you see yourself contributing to Shanghai's culinary scene?

Chef Fukui:
I'd like to develop a Shanghai cuisine of a new form. A form that is fusion, yet not mere fusion food. I'd like my food to represent a perfect world and a new Shanghai.

Shanghainese Crab, Avocado and Celeriac Timbale Salad with Aromatic Balsamic Sauce accompanied by Beluga Caviar

INGREDIENTS

Julienne of celeriac
30g, cut into 5-cm strips

Julienne of apple
5g, cut into 5-cm strips

Mayonnaise
10g

Shanghainese crabmeat
50g

Diced tomatoes
40g, cut into 1-cm squares

Diced avocado
40g, cut into 1-cm squares

Beluga caviar
10g

Veal stock
50ml

Pommery mustard
50g

Olive oil
50ml

Mixed greens

Cherry tomatoes, yellow and red

Radish
4-5 slices

Dill
a sprig

Seasoning:

Tamari soy sauce
100ml

Balsamic vinegar
1 litre

Garlic
25g

Dried juniper berry
4g

Dried thymes
5g

Dried bay leaves
3g

Black pepper
5g

White pepper
5g

Green pepper
5g

Pink pepper
4g

METHOD

- Mix the celeriac, apples and mayonnaise well.

- Place a timbale case of 6.5cm width and 3.5cm height on a plate and fill it with equal layers of crabmeat, diced tomatoes, diced avocado and the celeriac and apple mixture.

- Press the filling with a teaspoon and remove the timbale case gently.

- Top the timbale salad with the Beluga caviar.

- Prepare the sauce by mixing and boiling the seasoning ingredients with 50ml of veal stock and reduce the heat. Leave it aside to cool, then add 50g of Pommery mustard and 50ml of olive oil.

- Garnish with the mixed greens, cherry tomatoes, radish and dill and drizzle with the prepared sauce.

Chef Qian Shixian

SOPHIA'S TEA & RESTAURANT
480 Huashan Lu

HE chemistry between a chef and his food
..... the chemistry of flavours... let the flame work
its chemistry... Chef Qian has probably heard
them all.

The intimate, domestic
setting of the restaurant;
Chef Qian in his very tiny
kitchen (opposite page,
top right).

That's because he fingered test tubes long before he tossed a wok. You see, Chef Qian is a chemist by education.

He admits he uses MSG sparingly in his food. "People are scared when they hear this term," Chef Qian goes on about monosodium glutamate —the dreaded MSG, "but I don't agree. It actually contains some nutrients that the human body needs. If you consume a little, it's actually good for you." Only an applied chemist would know that, I thought, as he would the fact that MSG reacts with high temperature to become toxic, making its introduction at a very early stage of cooking imperative.

All very impressive, but what I'm interested to know is—can he cook?

Like a culinary Einstein it seems!

Chef Qian is a leading practitioner of *haipai* cuisine, the so-considered new wave of Shanghai cuisine. This style is revisionist and minimalist in its objectives, and moves from its heavy-flavoured and oil-laced roots to an altogether

The sweet fermented rice dessert (top left); the arduous task of extracting crabmeat (top right); the so-familiar concentration once again (bottom); having a pinch of the Crabmeat with Tofu behind the backs of the chefs (opposite page).

fresher, lighter and healthier palate. It's the 'pure originality' that Chef Qian aspires to—the emphasis on intrinsic flavours of the ingredients through the avoidance of heavy seasoning and cooking. In this, Chef Qian's academic understanding of chemical interaction puts him in almost unique advantage over all other master chefs.

And while his approach may appear empirical and almost quasi-scientific, his apprenticeship couldn't be more traditional. It is the classic mentor-protégé relationship of Chinese lore, the mentor here being Chef Qian's father-in-law, the famed Chef Xu Zhengcai. His awakening from complete culinary 'darkness', Chef Qian laughs, began with his first mouthful of his father-in-law's cooking.

Chef Xu introduced *haipai* cuisine to Shanghainese dining in the eighties, a style his 43-year-old son-in-law today develops and refines, and serves at his restaurant, Sophia's Tea & Restaurant. With its relaxed, intimate ambience, exquisitely fresh ingredients, and *haipai* menu with roots in the regional cuisines south of the Yangtze River, as well as Beijing, Szechuan and even modern Hong Kong, the restaurant has gained a devoted following among discerning Shanghainese and foreigners, and attracted media interest overseas.

So while Chef Qian headlines Sophia's Tea & Restaurant, Chef Xu reigns supreme at its chic, fine-dining companion-restaurant at Huaihai Lu's Times Square mall.

The mantle of his father-in-law is unquestionably on Chef Qian's shoulders now, and it bears repeating—there *is* chemistry between the chef and his food!

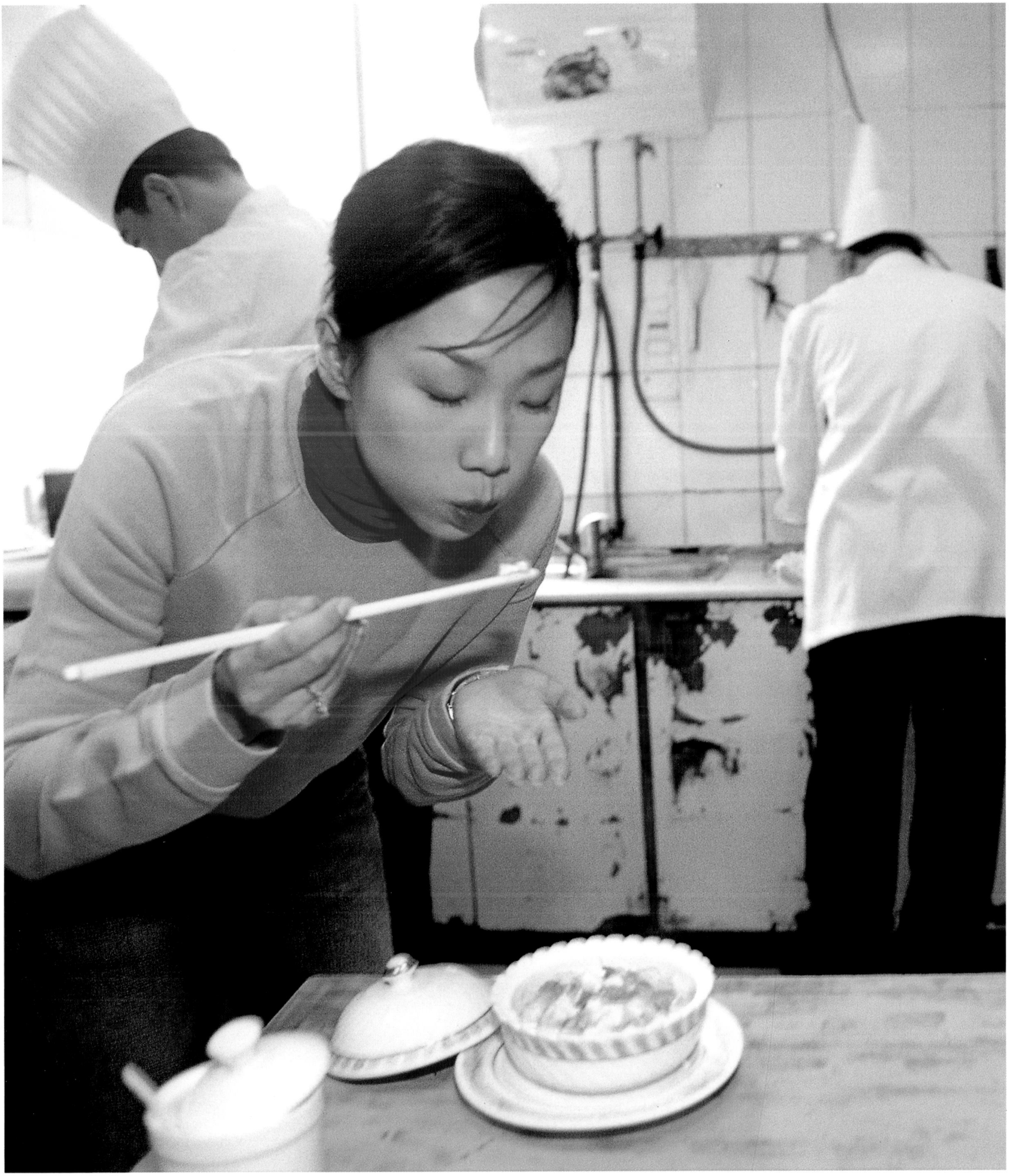

"Our movements when we cook should be minimal. We try not to stir or turn the food too much. If it can be done in one step, do it in one, not two."

– Chef Qian Shixian

Table talk

Sandy:
What's your attitude towards food?

Chef Qian:
It's a simple attitude. Food must be fresh, good for your health and tasty at the same time. It should be obtained in an environmentally friendly manner. My attitude towards cooking is similar. Food should be cooked so that it is *se xiang wei ju quan* (encompasses the qualities of colour, fragrance and taste) and *yuan zi yuan wei* (original flavour).

Sandy:
What inspires you?

Chef Qian:
First, I want to qualify that everyone has limitations; we can't be continuously creative. Inspiration occasionally comes in a flash, and if you grab hold of the opportunity, you might produce something creative. But the most important thing is to work hard. You need to learn and relearn things, charge and recharge your mind and be knowledgeable—even in literature, philosophy and art. Even something as simple as the humble soy sauce can inspire you if you study it thoroughly.

Crabmeat with Tofu

INGREDIENTS

Cooking oil
1 tsp

Freshwater crabmeat
25g

Crab roe
25g

Diced tofu
200g

Clear stock or chicken broth
1 Tbsp

Seasoning:

Millet wine or rice wine
1 tsp

Salt
$^1/_2$ tsp

Cornflour
1 tsp

Pepper
to taste

METHOD

- Heat oil in wok and fry the crabmeat and crab roe till fragrant.

- Add wine, diced tofu and clear stock. Simmer for two minutes.

- Add salt and cornflour and mix well.

- Pour it out into a bowl and add pepper to taste before serving.

Rose-Petal Prawns

INGREDIENTS

Freshwater prawns
200g

Fresh rose petals
12 pieces

Egg white

Seasoning:

Cooking oil
2 tsp

Salt
$^1/_4$ tsp

Cornstarch
15g

METHOD

- Wash the prawns.

- Dab the prawns dry with a clean piece of cloth. Marinate in a mixture of salt, egg white, cornstarch and mix well. Leave in the fridge for half an hour.

- Wash the rose petals in clean water and leave them aside to dry.

- Heat oil in wok. Heat should be medium. Add prawns and fry till almost done. Add cornstarch, stirring quickly. Add rose petals. Remove and serve quickly.

Lion's Head with Crabmeat

INGREDIENTS

Marbled pork with
70 percent lean meat and
30 percent fat, 250g

Fresh crabmeat
20g

Crab roe
20g

Mustard greens
few stalks, blanched

Seasoning:

Salt
1 tsp

Clear stock or chicken broth
1 tsp

METHOD

- Wash the pork clean. Chop it coarsely, to the size of green beans.

- Add crabmeat and crab roe and 1 tsp of clear stock and mix well until mixture turns sticky.

- Add salt and mix until pork has a springy texture.

- Shape pork into meatballs and steam for five minutes.

- Serve with mustard greens.

Uncle Li

SHANGHAI UNCLE
211 Tianyue Lu, 2nd floor
500 Zhangyang Lu, Time Square,
8th floor, Pudong

T'S hard not to notice TK Li.

He's a bear of a man with a booming rasp of a voice. He spews Cantonese, Shanghainese and English all at once, wears a bristly buzz cut and coloured suspenders that make him look not a day over 55 (he's really 75!), and has packed more living into his life than most people do in several lifetimes. When Uncle Li, as he's affectionately known, is in the room, the conversation never flags, never falters.

Uncle Li beams as I scoop the beef curry, which is his own original creation prepared from a multitude of spices.

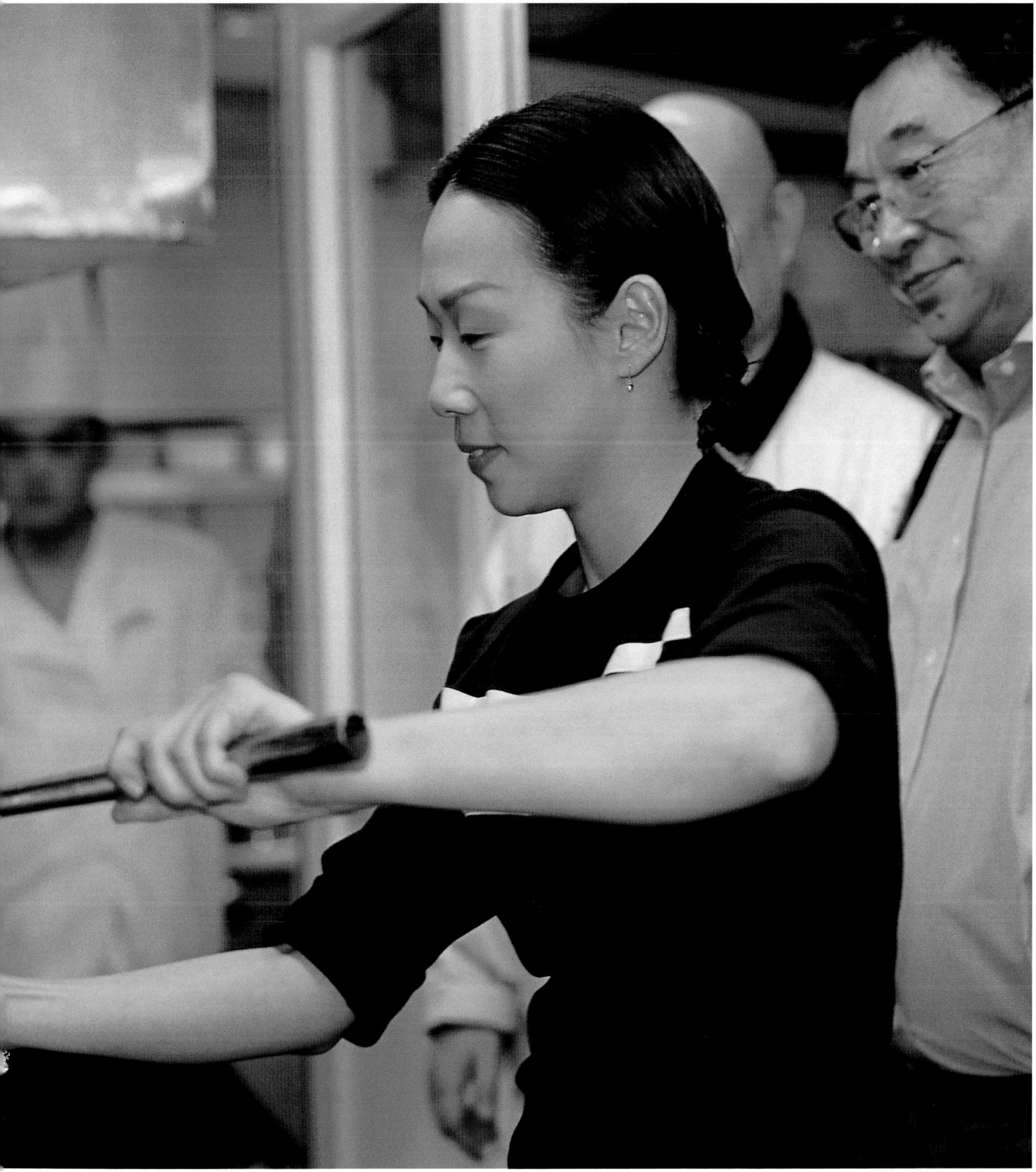

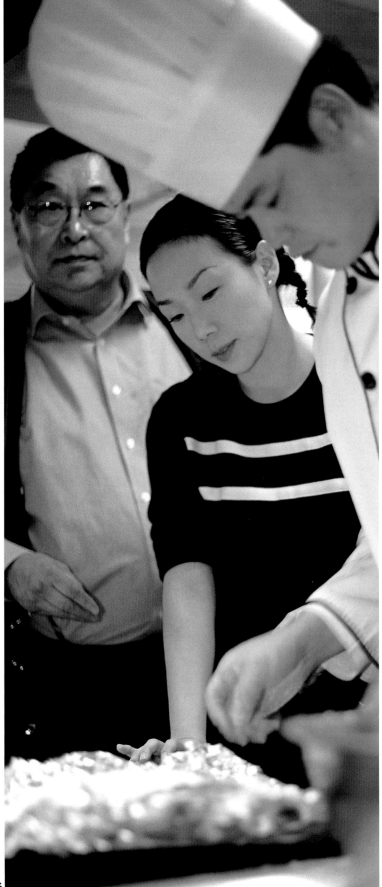

It doesn't have a chance to.

That's because the man is a good old-fashioned raconteur; and the tales he tells are all the more compelling because he's lived them.

Uncle Li traces his lineage to the powerful Qing Dynasty bureaucrat Li Tengzhang. In 1937, he moved with his wealthy family from Shanghai—where he was born—to Hong Kong to escape the war.

He was educated in India, Hong Kong, China and the United States, where he earned a PhD in physics from the University of California in Berkeley.

He returned to China in the 1950s, was persecuted by the government and imprisoned for some 20 years. He later spent 13 years in the South Pacific where he learned the finer points of French cuisine, went back again to Hong Kong to set up 11 restaurants with 2,700 employees, including almost 500 chefs. At the peak of his fortunes, he sold all the restaurants and returned to his birthplace, Shanghai, where he now owns the Shanghai Uncle restaurant, one of the finest and most famous restaurants in the city.

How's that for a story! You should hear it from the Uncle himself...

On the extensive menu at Shanghai Uncle are 38 tantalisingly termed 'Uncle Specials', each—hardly surprisingly—with a tale of its own. A favourite of Uncle Li's is the one about the recipe for smoked fish—a traditional but increasingly uncommon Shanghainese dish—and how he got it.

The Uncle's mother loved the smoked fish at a restaurant, Lao Dafang, so much she paid one tael of gold to its chef to have him over at her kitchen for two days to teach her. The smoked fish is today Shanghai Uncle's renowned signature dish. In fact many of the dishes at Shanghai Uncle originated from that same kitchen, which, at one time, had seven chefs, each with his own speciality. Uncle Li didn't quite elaborate on the mysterious acquisition of those other recipes—but I'm sure he'll pick one fine day to tell me.

Given the full and exciting life he's had, Uncle Li knows the value of knowledge—and its importance to excellence in whatever one does. He believes a chef who lacks knowledge of his craft will never produce great food. So each day, the head chef of the restaurant sits through two hours of history and geography! He might learn about, say, curry and its origins, and the climatic conditions of India. All this so a diner will be served Uncle Li's beef curry cooked to perfection.

With Alex, the manager of the restaurant

> ## "Whatever I put on the table must be the best of its kind."
> – Uncle Li

Sandy:
What's the difference between Chinese and Western cooking?

Uncle Li:
The Chinese emphasise the actual cooking, while Western cooking is about the sauce. The sauce for a Western dish can take up to 1 1/2 hours to prepare while Chinese cooks rely largely on soy sauce. Both the French and the Chinese both go to extremes in their cuisine—but they both aim for the best. To the French, however, documenting their food in recipes is important, while the Chinese prefer to do it to taste.

Sandy:
What are your principles when it comes to operating your restaurant?

Uncle Li:
Let me use designer labels as an example. The worker who produces the clothes is merely carrying out the orders of the designer. Chinese restaurants operate much like this, where workers take orders from the chef, who controls the kitchen. If the chef leaves, the restaurant is left in a lurch. In Western countries, many owners of gourmet restaurants are themselves the chefs. And that's the arrangement here—the owner is the designer, like myself, and the main chef is like my engineer.

Soy Sauce-flavoured Fried Grass Carp

INGREDIENTS

Grass carp
800g

Oil
for deep-frying

Marinade:

Dark soy sauce
1 Tbsp

Salt
1 tsp

Wine
$^1/_2$ tsp

Dip:

Star anise
4 segments

Cinnamon stick
1

Spring onion
4 stalks

Ginger
4 slices

Dark soy sauce
1 Tbsp

Sugar
1 Tbsp

Water
4 Tbsp

Note: A 4kg fish is the best weight for cutting into good-sized slices.

METHOD

- Use only the middle section of the carp. Cut this section into slices and marinate the fish slices in the prepared marinade for 2 hours.

- Remove fish slices and leave each individual piece to dry for about 3 hours.

- Heat oil in wok until hot and fry fish until crisp.

- For the dip, mix the ingredients thoroughly and heat over low fire. When the sauce thickens slightly, remove from the heat. Leave the fish slices in this mixture for more than 5 minutes to absorb the flavours then remove and leave to dry.

- Serve immediately.

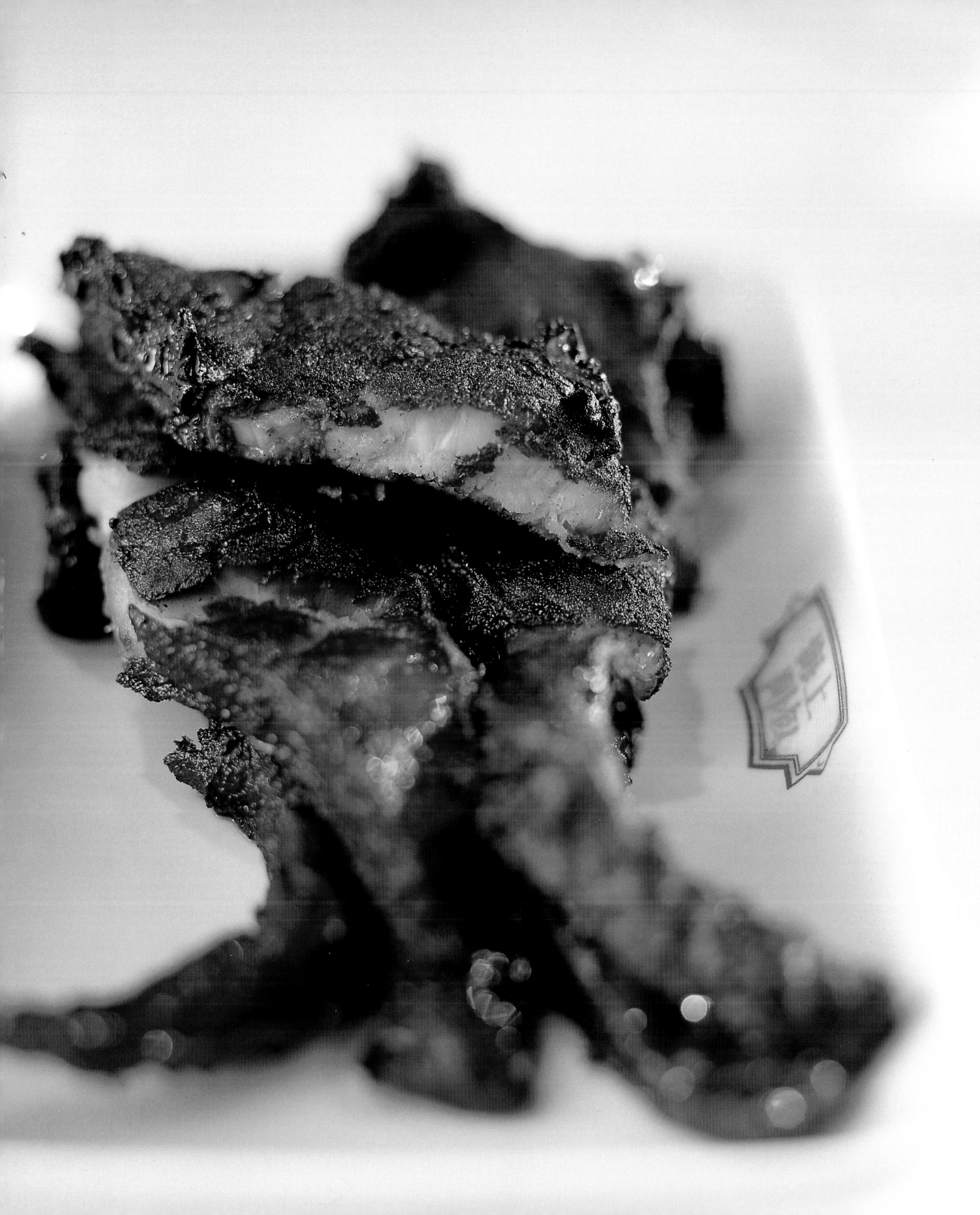

Stewed Pork Belly with Garlic

INGREDIENTS

Pork belly
1kg, cut into square pieces

Garlic
2kg (whole)

Salt
to taste

METHOD

- Use about 1kg of top quality pork belly. Scald in boiling water then remove bone and trim.

- Steam pork until nearly done.

- Transfer to a small claypot. Add a little water and cover meat with 2kg garlic. Season to taste with salt.

- Stew over low heat until garlic is soft. It takes about 1 hour to flavour the meat.

- Remove and transfer to lotus leaf and serve.

Salt-baked Mandarin Fish

INGREDIENTS

Mandarin fish
800g

Fermented wine paste
50g

Salt
2kg

METHOD

- Preheat oven to 200°C.

- Prepare the fresh fish. Cut and clean thoroughly. Remove bones.

- Stuff the small packet of fermented wine paste into fish belly and wrap the entire fish with muslin.

- Cover muslin-wrapped fish with damp salt and bake at 180°C for 40 minutes.

- Break open salt crust.

- Serve fish immediately.

Glossary

Bamboo shoots
These cream-coloured shoots are available canned or fresh. If using fresh, peel away the dark outer skin to reveal the heart. Fresh bamboo shoots require prolonged boiling.

Beancurd sheet, Hangzhou
A local speciality of Hangzhou, it is also known as Fuyang bean curd sheets.

Beancurd sheets
These thin, pale, translucent sheets are formed by boiling soy bean milk. The skin that forms on the surface is carefully removed and dried to form beancurd sheets. Wipe with a damp cloth or soak in water for about 10 minutes to soften before use.

Beef shank
The front leg of the animal, beef shank is full of tendons and the meat is tough. Thus, it must be slowly stewed or braised for the meat to be tender.

Breadcrumbs, dried
Dried and powdered breadcrumbs can be purchased from the supermarket. It is used in cooking to coat food before deep-frying or as a topping for certain dishes.

Cabbage, Beijing
A compact cabbage with crinkled-edged leaves. This tender and succulent vegetable keeps well and can be cooked in a variety of ways. Choose cabbages that are heavy for its size, with firmly packed, crisp-looking leaves.

Cabbage, snow
A leafy vegetable with a flavour similar to spinach. It is salt-pickled or eaten fresh. The pickled version can be purchased in cans at Chinese supermarkets or grocers, and is often used as an ingredient in stir-fried and braised dishes.

Caviar, beluga
One of the three main types of caviar. This expensive fish roe is from the beluga sturgeon of the Caspian Sea. Beluga caviar boasts large pea-sized eggs that range in colour from silvery-black to black.

Crab, freshwater hairy
Hairy crabs mature between the months of September and December and can be found in almost every Chinese restaurant in Shanghai during this period. Hairy crabs were originally from the Yang Cheng Lake in China and those harvested from this lake are still touted to be the best-tasting ones.

Carp, grass
Native to East Asia, it inhabits rivers, ponds and ricefields. Its meat is said to have a strong algal flavour but it is regarded as the most palatable of all Asian carps.

Chicken broth
Made by simmering chicken and water, this broth is flavourful and tasty. Ready-made broth can be purchased from supermarkets.

Cinnamon stick
The bark of the cinnamon tree, available in thin quills. Used to flavour both savoury and sweet dishes, as well as drinks.

Coriander
Also known as cilantro or Chinese parsley, this green leafy herb, especially the roots, imparts a distinctive pungent flavour to dishes. It is commonly used as a garnish. Do not substitute with other types of parsley.

Fermented wine paste
A reddish wine paste made with cooked glutinous rice and red rice.

Five-spice powder
A reddish-brown coloured spice powder consisting of a mix of ground star anise, fennel, cinnamon, cloves and Sichuan pepper. Five-spice powder is used in many Chinese dishes. As with all spices, it will lose its flavour over time, so do not store too long.

Flour, glutinous rice
Made from glutinous rice, this flour is more elastic than ordinary wheat flour. It becomes clear and sticky when cooked. Glutinous rice flour is commonly used to make the dough for Chinese dim sum dishes.

Garoupa
A member of the seabass family, garoupa is also known as groupa. This fish has firm sweet, tasty flesh. Garoupa is suitable for steaming, frying, braising and even baking. A common variety used in Chinese cooking is the red garoupa.

Goose liver (foie gras)
A highly-prized delicacy. Foie gras is the enlarged liver of a goose or duck force-fed and methodically fattened over a period of a few months.

Ham, Chinese
A leg of cured pork used to enhance flavour in soups and dishes. The most famous Chinese ham is from Yunnan, hence Chinese ham is sometimes synonymously called Yunnan ham.

Lard
Made from processed pork fat, lard is flavourful when used for frying. Its soft texture also makes for light and fluffy cakes and pastries when used in baking.

Lily buds
Also known as golden needles, lily buds lend an earthy flavour to many dishes. They are usually softened by soaking in warm water, then tied into a knot before use.

Mandarin fish
Also called 'osmanthus fish'. It belongs to the seabass family but lives in fresh water. This fish has a long head, large mouth and pretty grey patterns on its body. It is favoured for its thick, tender flesh and high nutritional value and is believed to alleviate rectal ulcers and diarrhoea.

Mayonnaise
A cold emulsified sauce consisting of egg yolks and oil blended together and flavoured with vinegar, salt, pepper and mustard.

Mushroom, black, dried
These dried fragrant mushrooms will keep almost indefinitely if kept in a clean, dry airtight jar. Soak for about 30 minutes to soften and trim stems before use.

Niangao, dried
Also known as Foochow rice cakes, since that is where they originated from. They are translucent white in colour and have a flat longish shape. Soak in water overnight to soften before use.

Oil, sesame
Pressed from roasted sesame seeds, this aromatic oil is used as a flavouring agent and an ingredient in sauces.

Oil, olive, virgin
Obtained from tree-ripened olives, olive oil is a mono-unsaturated oil. Its flavour and colour varies, depending on the crop of olives, the region and the grade. Virgin olive oil is a first-press oil.

Osmanthus blossoms, dried
Also known as *gui hua,* these dried flowers are sprinkled over sweet soups and cakes for their fragrance. Osmanthus flowers are said to improve digestion.

Oyster sauce
A thick brown sauce with a rich flavour. Made from oyster extract and flavoured with seasoning. Commonly used in stir-fries.

Prawns, freshwater
There are many varieties of freshwater prawns and they vary in size from small to large. Freshwater prawns have firm flesh and a sweet flavour when cooked. They are generally grayish in colour and turn orange-pink when cooked.

Preserved vegetables
Also known as *mei cai,* these are cooked mustard vegetables that are steeped in a salt and sugar solution, and then dried. Wash well to get rid of excess salt and any sediment before cooking.

Sauce, soy (dark and light)
A popular ingredient used in Chinese cooking. Prepared from fermented soy beans, sauce soy comes in two varieties—dark and light. Dark soy sauce is used not only for its salty flavour, but also to add colour to dishes. Light soy sauce flavours food without changing the colour of the dish. It is also commonly used as a condiment.

Sauce, soy (Tamari)
Tamari is the traditional Japanese soy, made with fermented soy beans and wheat. It is darker in colour and flavour than soy sauce, and is often used as a dip for tempura and sushi.

Soy bean, green
An edible soy bean that produces clusters of pods with green beans. In China and most Asian countries, the beans are cooked with meat or mixed with other vegetables in various dishes. The pods can be frozen for future use.

Spring onions
Also known as scallions, these are onions that have small bulbs and long green stalks. They are usually added raw into dishes for flavour or used as garnish.

Star anise
An eight-pointed, star-shaped spice, star anise is favoured for its scent. Store in an airtight jar to preserve its flavour. It is one of the five spices that make up five-spice powder.

Starch (potato and wheat)
Flours made from grains and tubers are commonly used as thickening agents in Chinese cooking.

Sugar, rock
Large irregularly shaped crystals of sugar used mainly in Chinese sweet soups or desserts.

Tabasco sauce
A hot sauce made from chilli peppers marinated in spirit vinegar and salt.

Tangerine peel
The dried rind of tangerines is used for flavouring sweet soups and desserts. It imparts a citrus-tangy flavour to dishes it is added to. It will keep indefinitely if stored in a clean, dry airtight container.

Truffles, monkey head
Monkey head mushrooms grow naturally on fallen forest logs. Cultivated in China and Japan for hundreds of years, they have a pungent, woody flavour and are useful for lowering cholesterol and regulating blood pressure.

Vermicelli, transparent
Also known as cellophane noodles, these dried noodles need to be soaked in hot water for 5 minutes before use. They do not have much flavour on their own, making them extremely suitable for adding into soups since they absorb liquids and flavours readily.

Vinegar, Balsamic
Of Italian origin, balsamic vinegar is made from white Trebbiano grape juice. It is dark in colour and has a pungent sweet flavour.

Vinegar, Changjiang and Zhengjiang
Vinegar is one of the oldest seasonings used in Asian cuisine. Both Changjiang and Zhengjian vinegars are dark vinegars. Changjiang vinegar is made from an assortment of rice and grains while Zhengjiang vinegar is made from glutinous rice.

Watercress
A vegetable with long fibrous stems and small leaflets. Choose the tender young green shoots, as the thick lower stems tend to be tough. Watercress can also be identified by the fine white roots found growing at the base of its leaves and shoots.

Wine, Hua Tiao
Chinese rice wine made from glutinous rice. Commonly used as a marinade in cooking.

Wine, rice
Chinese rice wine is known as *shaosing* and is amber-coloured with a rich, sweetish taste.

Wonton skins
These thin square sheets of dough can be bought from the supermarkets. Once open, wrap them back tightly or cover with a damp cloth to prevent them from drying out. Once dried, these skins cannot be used for wrapping dumplings.

Yellow croaker
A low fat fish with dark blotches on its back and spots on the upper body. It has firm dark flesh that is moist and mild-tasting. May be substituted with sea trout.

Special thanks to:

David Yip
Joanne Sun
Marjo Yim
Chef Jereme Leung
Chef Susumu Fukui
Chef Qian Shixian
Paul Hsu
Uncle Li
Ah Niang
Madam He Shuiying
Tan Dawn Wei and Stephen Lee, writers
Gina Lau, hairstylist
Clarence Lee, makeup artist
Fang Chi-Lun, fashion stylist
BOSS...HUGO BOSS, CLUB 21 and
  DKNY, for the wardrobe
Xiao Ji, cooking assistant
Pu Dong Kitchen, Singapore
Gourmet Haven, Singapore